## Praise for *The Angel Experiment*

"In her new book, *The Angel Experiment*, Corin Grillo will open your eyes and your heart to the unknown world of angel guidance and transformation through Spirit. Her lively and love-filled book will inspire you to take your life to a new level and to find deeper meaning in your everyday experiences. Corin has helped countless people move to a new level in their lives by introducing them to their angels and to the more meaningful and lasting world of Spirit. Bravo, Corin!"

— *Meredith Young-Sowers*, DDiv, author of
*Angelic Messenger Cards, Agartha, Wisdom Bowls,*
and *Spirit Heals* and cofounder of the
Stillpoint School and Foundation

"Corin Grillo offers a practical, actionable, and powerful way to work with mystical forces that are very real — and very much want to help you! Her enthusiasm for, and commitment to, opening others to angels and divine guidance is infectious and will inspire readers everywhere."

— *Tanya Carroll Richardson*, professional intuitive
and author of *Angel Intuition, Angel Insights,*
*Zen Teen,* and *Are You an Earth Angel?*

"Corin Grillo is the real deal when it comes to working with the divine. She is a bridge between the angelic and human realms, an⌐ ⌐⌐ delivers insights with a ton of love in a humor⌐ ⌐ way. Here she lays out angelic realm and guides you on an intimate journey to a life where the miraculous is an everyday experience. If the title even slightly intrigues you, you are going to love this beautifully grounded and wise book!"

— *Lee Harris*, author of *Energy Speaks*

"Corin Grillo has written a winner. I love her down-to-earth approach to angels and the roles they play in our lives. The timing of *The Angel Experiment* is perfect. This book will bring so much peace of mind, heart, and soul to the millions searching for answers right now. Congratulations, Corin, on writing such a beautiful, loving, thought-provoking book."

— *Echo Bodine*, author of *Echoes of the Soul*

"Angels are just one call away! Corin Grillo brings clarity to the magic of angel healing in every area of your life and will inspire you to take steps immediately for divine serendipity. Simple, easy, and oh, so powerful!"

— *Jean Slatter*, author of *Hiring the Heavens* and founder of the Higher Guidance Life Coach program and the Creative Mystic program

# THE
# ANGEL
# EXPERIMENT

# THE
# ANGEL
## EXPERIMENT

## A 21-Day
## Magical Adventure to
## Heal Your Life

—————— ⚜ ——————

## CORIN GRILLO

New World Library
Novato, California

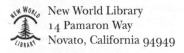

New World Library
14 Pamaron Way
Novato, California 94949

Text design by Tona Pearce Myers

Library of Congress Cataloging-in-Publication Data

Names: Grillo, Corin, date, author.
Title: The angel experiment : a 21-day magical adventure to heal your life / Corin Grillo.
Description: Novato, California : New World Library, 2019. | Summary: "A contemporary approach to the age-old practice of calling on angels for assistance; the author describes experiments that allow readers to 'test' the power of angels, step-by-step, over 21 days"— Provided by publisher.
Identifiers: LCCN 2019022223 (print) | LCCN 2019981529 (ebook) | ISBN 9781608686254 (print : alk. paper) | ISBN 9781608686261 (ebook)
Subjects: LCSH: Angels. | Spiritual life. | Spiritual healing. | Mental healing.
Classification: LCC BL477 .G76 2019 (print) | LCC BL477 (ebook) | DDC 202/.15—dc23
LC record available at https://lccn.loc.gov/2019022223
LC ebook record available at https://lccn.loc.gov/2019981529

First printing, October 2019
ISBN 978-1-60868-625-4
Ebook ISBN 978-1-60868-626-1
Printed in Canada on 100% postconsumer-waste recycled paper

New World Library is proud to be a Gold Certified Environmentally Responsible Publisher. Publisher certification awarded by Green Press Initiative.

10   9   8   7   6   5   4   3

*For Jack, Lucia, and Luna — the most amazing*
*and ridiculous humans I know.*
*Your love and support have*
*meant the world to me.*

———————— ❧ ————————

# Contents

# Introduction

Don't blame me for this book. The angels told me to write it.

Over the years I've learned to listen to them because when I do, miracles happen — literally.

I'm guessing you're here for one of two reasons. Maybe you're just curious about angels and want to learn more about them. Or perhaps you're in a place in life where you could use a heavy dose of divine intervention. In either case, you're in for a real treat.

Over the next 21 days, you will enter the magical world of angels.

Some people think of angels as being sweet, loving, heavenly beings who sit around all day singing and playing the harp, but I can assure you, they are much more than that. They are also powerful allies who are here to help you, and right now they are waiting on standby, ready to help you manifest the health, wealth, love, and life of your dreams.

When you invite the divine to help you in your

life daily, you are seizing an incredible opportunity to receive additional support, deep healing, and expedited manifestations of pure goodness. By enlisting the angels to come to your aid, you are hiring the most powerful army known to humankind to whip your life into shape in beautiful, magical, and even miraculous ways.

This book is based on a 21-day angel course called "The 21 Days of Angelmas" that I first offered back in 2015 and released to an international audience. This course provides a nonreligious yet highly spiritual step-by-step method of working with the angels.

It's fun, it's easy — and even better, it actually works.

After its first release, the results were overwhelming. People began reporting profound healing on all levels of their being and in their lives: chronic physical conditions greatly improving and often disappearing altogether, addictions vanishing, panic attacks stopping, depression dissolving, new job offers coming in, excessive amounts of joy and hope bubbling up for the first time in years...and the list goes on.

One of the most beautiful things that happens for people when they do these 21 days with the angels is that they develop a deep connection with their angels and with their higher power (*God, Source, Creator,* or whatever name feels right). A palpable relationship is created in which people report actually being able to see and feel the presence of angels.

Right now, you may be asking yourself, "Does this stuff really work? Are angels even real? Is this all BS?"

Healthy skepticism is 100 percent welcome. I used to be a skeptic myself, until the angels threw an earth-shattering miracle my way. After that, I just couldn't deny their existence anymore.

And I want the same thing to happen for you. I don't want you to just take my word for it that angels are real. I want you to experience the reality of angels for yourself.

That being said, treat this book as if you are a scientist beginning a potentially groundbreaking laboratory experiment. This laboratory just happens to be your own life.

Keep an open mind and pay attention to every detail of each day's instructions. Commit to completing this 21-day journey, and when you're done, decide for yourself!

This just might turn out to be the most important experiment of your life.

Last, but definitely not least, I want to tell you that just by opening this book and reading these first few pages, you have already let the angels know you are curious about them. Because of this, things can begin shifting for you right away, so keep your eyes peeled for extra doses of goodness and synchronicities coming your way.

Welcome aboard this 21-day angel adventure. The angels are excited to show you just how real they are.

# PART I

---　❧　---

# ANGEL
# BASICS

---　❧　---

# Miracles Are Real

Do you believe in miracles? I didn't, until one happened to me several years ago. It wasn't just a casual miracle. It was a miracle that completely shattered the foundation of my education as a licensed psychotherapist and what I thought it meant to be a rational and grounded human being.

This miracle happened in a place where I least expected it, yet at a time when I needed it most. It catapulted me into a life that is utterly different from my earlier one — in a good way.

I am still in awe of the amazing ways that the angels continue to show their love and support, not just to me but to the incredible people I work with all around the world. I'm excited to share with you what I've learned about the angels and to show you how to powerfully contact them to come to your aid in the mind-blowing ways that they often do. When the angels enter your life, it's rarely subtle, but it's always healing, loving, and even miraculous, no matter what you are struggling with.

I know this because over the years I have witnessed jaw-dropping, undeniable proof of the presence and power of the angels in my own life and in the lives of my clients — miracle after miracle.

For the first 37 years of my life, I suffered from chronic depression. I use the phrase *my life* loosely — I was the walking dead. I white-knuckled my way through life pretending to be happy, but on the inside I was tortured, and my only true prayer each morning was for that day to be my last.

On the outside, I put on a great show: I had a house, a child, a great husband, a prestigious education, and an incredible career. I was living the American dream, yet it wasn't enough.

I was missing something — something big. Yet no matter what I did, nothing seemed to help. You know what else hadn't helped? An early life that was full of abuse, poverty, profound loss, drug addiction, and alcohol, and even included a wee stint in jail.

When I was younger, the shit got deep for me fast, and even though I managed to put those darker years behind me and "make something of myself," the shadows of my past still haunted me, nagging for my attention.

It turned out that I was great at surviving, but I sucked at thriving. Hence the white-knuckling. I wanted it all to end, but I was too much of a wuss to take my own life.

Little did I know that the end was in fact quite near, but not in the way that I was hoping.

A bona fide, earth-shattering miracle was on its way, and it was about to change everything.

## You Are Not Alone

Before I tell you about the incredible miracle that happened to me on that monumental day, I want you to know that this book isn't really about me. It's about you. It's about the incredible healing and miracles that can happen for you, if you just learn how to let the angels into your life.

It's about how the exact steps that you'll learn have already helped and healed thousands of people all over the world.

And it's also about three of the biggest points that I have learned from working with the angels:

Point #1: You are not alone.

Point #2: There is no such thing as coincidence.

Point #3: Miracles are real.

Your angels are constantly guiding you in your everyday life, leading you to the people, places, and things that will help you heal your life in amazing ways. I believe that the angels brought you here today so that you too can learn how to work with them and enlist their miraculous help in whatever parts of your life that need it most.

There is no problem too big or too small for the

angels. They want to help you in every aspect of your life. They want to help you with your health, your wealth, your love life, your life purpose, your relationships, your family, and so much more.

And all you have to do is just one thing: you must learn how to ask for their help in a consistent and powerful way. Soon you will learn how.

In just five to ten minutes each day for 21 days, the guided daily meditations and invocations in this book will open you up to the reality that angels exist and that in specific and palpable ways they can help you manifest a life that is beyond your wildest dreams.

## Are Angels Real?

Angels aren't just paintings on the ceilings of fancy cathedrals or characters in ancient religious books. They're real allies that can do amazing things for you.

For thousands of years, indigenous peoples, as well as all the major religions of the world, have talked about benevolent beings sent from God/Source/ Creator to aid humankind. Christianity, Judaism, Buddhism, Hinduism, and Islam all agree on at least one thing: that powerful beings of light exist and are here to help humanity.

Angels are for everyone in all walks of life. You don't have to follow any particular religion in order for them to help you. The fact that you have never seen an angel, or that an angel hasn't shown up at your front door playing a harp and offering you a sandwich, doesn't mean that they aren't real. The angels find other creative ways to show you just how real they are, but if you aren't attuned to how angels influence your life, you will miss their signs.

Once you learn how to open your eyes in just the right way, you will begin seeing the indescribable angel magic that is happening around you all day long.

Once your spiritual eyes are open, your life will become a magical playground full of love, hope, support, and, yes, miracles.

## You Are Worthy

I used to think that because I wasn't religious or didn't go to church, I wasn't allowed to call upon the divine for support. I was wrong, and I want you to know that if you are judging yourself for who you are, if you feel like you don't have the right to enlist the help of the divine, then you are wrong too.

Every time I work with angels to help heal others or myself, I have learned that the angels (or God/ Source/Creator) don't judge us. They love prostitutes and princesses, sadists and Samaritans alike. The angels understand how difficult it is to be human. They understand the pain that we endure in human form, and they don't judge us for our fumbles or for the choices we make in order to survive.

To the angels you are a beautiful, innocent child. When a child falls when he is learning how to walk, does a loving mother smack her baby upside the head and call him stupid? Nope. She gently helps her cute, chubby baby back to his feet, gives him a loving squeeze, and encourages him to keep trying, absolutely knowing that he will get it right soon. To her he is absolute perfection, especially in his imperfection.

That's how the angels love humans. The angels have nothing but love and compassion for you.

So I want you to know in advance that you are worthy of the insane amounts of love, compassion, and healing that they have to offer. It doesn't matter if you don't go to church, are having rampant sexcapades, or are in the throes of full-blown addiction.

The angels love you just the same, and they want you to feel their love and support more than anything, no matter how you are feeling about yourself.

## What Will Change?

By doing this 21-day ritual with the angels, you can change any aspect of your life. Much of what changes is that you start feeling magically better, more hopeful and inspired, even if your life hasn't changed much on the outside. But that's not all.

Here's what else can be enhanced through these potent days with the angels:

- Your relationships can become healed and more harmonious.
- Your cash flow can open up.
- Your mental health can be restored.
- Your physical health and chronic conditions can vastly improve.
- Your intuitive and healing gifts can open up.
- You can attract soulmate relationships.

- You can heal from grief.
- Your life purpose and divine mission can become clearer.

Full-blown, jaw-dropping miracles and angel encounters become possible. And so much more — they are angels, after all.

There are specific angels to help you with everything under the sun, and soon you will learn about some of the main archangels. These archangels are the ones that came to me to create this 21-day angel ritual.

### Art and Science

Learning to work with angels is both an art and a science.

Learning to work properly with the angels to heal your life is essential; however, learning to see the miraculous footprints that angels leave behind in their divine wake is equally important. You will need to develop the right kind of eyes to see their signs, and that's exactly what you will do on this angel adventure. You will learn the art of not just believing in angels but experiencing their presence with your own senses.

I have no interest in trying to convince you that angels are real based on my word alone. I want you to find out for yourself, with your own eyes and ears, exactly just how real they are, like a scientist proving or disproving a hypothesis. Over these 21 days, your experience will matter more than anything, but it is imperative that you keep an open mind and keep solid records of your experiences along the way. That's where the science comes in.

I invite you to begin thinking of angels not as celestial beings chilling out in heaven or somewhere far away but a little differently. I want you to imagine that they are right here, standing in the room with you right now. Like good old friends gathered around you.

Say hello to them and let them know you are excited to work with them. It might feel odd at first, but please do it anyway. The sooner you make conscious contact with your angels, the sooner your angel magic will begin flowing.

Treat this book as the most important experiment of your life. Your new, miraculously healed and beautiful life could be waiting for you on the other side.

## What You Will Learn

Here is a brief outline of what you will learn:

- A powerful way to talk to angels so that they can hear you and help you
- How to hear, see, and feel the angels in your life
- How to create a daily ritual of inviting angels into your life
- Which specific archangels will help you manifest more cash, more love, more peace, and more protection
- 21 daily angel prayers/invocations that will help you open the door to manifesting miracles

- 21 healing meditations that will heal and detox your heart, mind, body, and soul, also available at TheAngelExperimentAudios.com as downloadable MP3s

So now I invite you to let go of everything you thought you knew about the world and about yourself, and make room for the possibility that everything in your life can be healed in miraculous ways through the help of the angels. From this point forward, anything is possible for you, miracles are real, and your angels are listening. Even the sky isn't the limit.

---- ❧ ----

# The First Miracle

Yes, I speak and teach about angels and spiritual healing to people for a living, but I wasn't always this way.

The miracle story that I am about to share with
you is so far beyond belief that it took me a few years
to share it with people. I thought they would think I
was crazy and put me on antipsychotics.

Since most of my friends at the time were, like me,
psychotherapists, I knew that if I told them about this
miracle, they would probably think it was "magical
thinking," a term used in the mental-health world that
is a red flag for psychosis. Not good.

But I knew I wasn't crazy, and even if I was, I had
every intention of continuing this path of madness,
because for the first time in my life...I felt joy. I felt
the presence of Spirit within me and around me, and
for the first time in a long time, I didn't feel alone.

This miracle had such a radical impact on my life
that it set me on a journey I could never have pre-
dicted.

It happened during a hard period in my life. My house was going into foreclosure, and my marriage was strained. I was working full-time for a county mental-health organization that assisted troubled teens in the ghettos of Los Angeles.

Since I'd lived in an LA ghetto as a teenager myself, working with children like this was near and dear to my heart, but it was also intense.

I went to children's homes to try to help them and their families. There were a lot of extreme clients in my caseload — children who were recovering from abuse, neglect, gang banging, suicide attempts, drugs, and so on.

The stress of the job was insane, and it was compounded by the fact that I had a beautiful four-year-old daughter at home who needed me. I'd gone from being a stay-at-home mom to working full-time almost overnight, and it was a horrific adjustment for us all. I never had time to myself, or for my family, and both my physical and mental health were suffering.

I was drinking too much and taking all kinds of prescription medications just to survive. I was burning the candle at both ends, and I felt like I was failing miserably at keeping my life together.

When my birthday came around, a friend of mine bought me an angel healing session as a gift. She had no idea how much I was suffering, but she bought this for me out of the "goodness of her heart."

Remember when I said there is no such thing as coincidence?

So I went to the angel healing not expecting

much, and 60 minutes later I felt like a completely different person.

I felt lighter, brighter, more hopeful, and connected to my spirit. I felt alive — quite possibly for the first time in my life. It was a miraculous experience, but not nearly as miraculous as what was to come.

## Meet the Angels

As I left the session, the healer told me to keep talking to my angels as if they were real, so that's what I did.

You see, I was not a religious person (I'm still not), I didn't go to church (still don't), I cussed like a sailor (still do), plus I had a long history of leading a not-so-pure lifestyle. These things, and many others, made me feel unworthy of divine love, so I never would have guessed that the angels would listen to someone like me. Perhaps you can relate?

Nonetheless, I did what she said. I experimented. Soon, it was as if the world itself had come to life and was communicating directly with me. Synchronicity after synchronicity. Trucks would drive by me with angel wings on the side of them. A license plate in front of me read "ANGL4U." I would turn on the radio, and no matter what station I happened to pick, there was a song playing about angels or with beautiful messages of love.

The angel synchronicities were coming at a rapid rate, so much so that I had absolutely no doubt that something real was happening, and it felt *big*. I began to feel their presence with me. I could feel them touching my hand and feel their love vibrating through my body. It was beautiful. I felt safe. I felt deeply loved, and this was simply not the normal feeling for me at the time!

Almost overnight, I went from feeling like I was a zombie to feeling like my life was a magical playground.

For two days this went on. Then came Day 3. On Day 3, I was driving in the *barrio* on my way to a client's home. Out of nowhere, a bird dropped from the sky and crash-landed on the ground directly in front of my car, so I slammed on the brakes.

It was broad daylight on a residential street when the bird landed. I wanted to step out of the car to help it, but because I was alone in a pretty dangerous part of town known for street violence, I decided it was best to stay in the car.

It was an awkward moment, to say the least. I looked closely at this beautiful little bird through my window and saw that one of its wings was completely mangled. It was struggling to get back up with its good wing, but no dice. Its wing was clearly too broken for flight.

My heart imploded as I realized that I would be late to my next client if I stopped to rescue the bird, so there was nothing I could really do for it in the amount of time I had. I remember shaking my fist at the angels and thinking, "Really, angels?! I have been talking to you for days, doing my best to call in good, loving vibes, and this is what I get? Bird carnage?!"

Feeling helpless, I decided to use my brand-new

trick. I decided to ask the angels for help. I asked them to surround the bird with love and healing and to take its pain away. I felt so terrible having to leave the bird, but this was the best I could do. So for a long moment I closed my eyes and sent good juju to the bird, asking the angels to take this bird out of its suffering.

I started to drive away, continuing to ask for help, and after I'd driven around the bird, I looked at the rearview mirror and noticed something peculiar. The bird was moving in a strange way. It started shaking on the ground. I stopped the car to continue to watch, and as I did, something incredible happened.

Before my eyes, I saw a tiny bird hop out of the bird's body and fly away. The suffering bird on the ground kept wiggling, and as it did, I saw a second tiny bird hop up and fly away from the body. Then a third bird that was a little smaller and darker than the other two jumped up and flew away. As the last bird flew away, I noticed that there was no bird body left on the ground. Zilch. Nada. Nothing. Much to my amazement, the bird with the mangled wing had completely transformed and vanished — right before my eyes.

At that point I forgot all about the client and the fact that I was in a dangerous neighborhood, and I got out of the car to see what the hell had just happened.

The bird was in fact gone.

The bird with a broken wing transformed into three healthy tiny birds and flew away. And it was in broad daylight. And I was in the ghetto. And most importantly, I was sober.

I felt the powerful presence of something beautiful around me. I had goose bumps up and down, and my heart exploded with a feeling that there are no words for except maybe *hallelujah*, if that word can describe an emotion.

It was some seriously *holy* shit. It was a miracle. And I saw it. And everything changed from that day forward.

## The Real Miracle

The bird wasn't the only one that received a miraculous healing that day. I did too. That day changed me. That day brought miraculous healing to my heart, my mind, my body, and my life, and it happened fast.

Watching a wounded bird divide itself into three healthy, flying birds was amazing, but the most profound miracle was the deep healing that happened in my life afterward. You see, like the body of the bird, the girl inside me, who for decades felt depressed, lost, and alone, also vanished. I could hear a new voice inside me. It was a nice voice, a loving voice that began leading me into a deeply fulfilling life full of purpose, love, abundance, and full-blown miracles.

That day, I began to live in a world where magic and miracles were not just possible, they were real, and they were happening frequently. Even wilder, my spiritual gifts began to unfold. My healing abilities and my intuition began to soar, and my life began to flow in ways that I had never known was possible. It was an awakening, and I was listening. I could finally hear the still, small voice inside me that was trying to set me free.

Slowly, step-by-step, and with incredible faith, I was guided into a life where I am now able to touch the lives of thousands of people all around the world. And to help them find their way back to their soul and spirit, so that they can also reclaim their own divine right to live a life full of purpose, love, hope, magic, and miracles.

Witnessing miracles never gets old, and since that very first miracle, I've seen so many more happen for myself and many others. It's been beyond incredible. And now I want a miracle for you.

## I'm Special and So Are You

What I didn't know then is that I had abilities and gifts inside me that were not obvious for decades of my life. I thought I knew who I was, but I didn't.

I didn't know a thing about the real me until I let the angels into my life to show me my path to freedom. And in that process, I discovered all kinds of hidden spiritual gifts that I didn't know were there.

So what I want you to know right now is that you have major gifts too. Your spiritual gifts could be completely different from mine, but they are there, and the more you work with the divine and your angels, the more you will discover the new, tricked-out divinity inside you that's just waiting to emerge.

That being said, if you think you know who you are

already...you just might not. There's more. There's always more, and it's beautiful.

All that's required to discover the goodness inside you is an authentic will to heal, to align your life with the divine, and to learn the best way to talk to angels so that they can hear you and you can hear them.

The next portion of the book will help you with just that. If you want to learn how to talk to angels and open your life to major goodness and transformation, the answers lie right ahead.

# How to Talk to Angels

Over the next 21 days, you will learn how to talk to angels. It is essential that you learn how to speak with them in such a way that they can clearly hear you, so that's what we'll cover in this section.

There are so many beautiful ways to communicate with your angels. You can share with them what you are worried about and ask them to help you with all kinds of things that you might be struggling with right now. You can talk to them casually all day long, whenever you are in the car, in the shower, meditating, or going to bed. Anytime is a good time to talk to angels.

As a matter of fact, you really don't even have to speak the words out loud. You can just think them, and they can still hear you. Angels are cool that way. Having heart-to-heart conversations with your angels throughout the day — whether out loud or just in your thoughts — is highly recommended, because amazing things can happen for you just from doing that.

Some people feel guilty about asking for help from the angels. If that is true for you, know that there's absolutely nothing to feel bad or guilty about. The good news is that angels absolutely love helping you! The bad news is that they really can't help you if you don't ask.

Humans have what's called *free will*. From my experience, the angels can't intervene and help you if you don't invite them into your life for support. Moral of the story? Ask, ask, ask, and then keep on asking.

## Prayer vs. Invocation

An invocation is a slightly more formal way to communicate with the angels. I am teaching it to you because it is the most powerful way that I know of to enlist their help.

Most people have heard the word *prayer*, but not too many people have heard of or understand the word *invocation*. I am going to focus on invocation because the energy of invocation is quite different from that of prayer and can be even more powerful.

Prayer is the act of calling upon a divinity outside yourself to intercede on your behalf to solve whatever problems you are having. Praying is an amazing way to connect with the divine and find peace and solace.

Invocation is outwardly similar to prayer. You are still calling on the divine for aid; however, an invocation actually invites the beautiful presence of the divine to fill your entire being, your heart, mind, body, and soul. To invoke is to essentially awaken and allow divinity to move through you, which, as you can imagine, can bring deep healing to all aspects of your being. The process of invocation includes you, a magical human, as one of the key ingredients of the recipe for miracle making. Prayer doesn't really do that.

Invocation acknowledges your own magic in the equation, and this is why I love using invocations and teaching about them.

### How to Do an Invocation

Even though the angels can completely hear you if you don't speak to them out loud, I find speaking invocations out loud helps you focus on your intentions, especially if your mind is all over the place.

When you're doing an invocation, you will want to get into the actual feeling and emotion of it. A solid invocation includes some level of passion or excitement. Find the *emotion* behind your request, because it's through your emotions that so much of your life becomes manifest. Do your best to excite yourself with passion. Some people do this by playing music, singing the invocation (more on this to come), or even dancing.

If you have ever heard Aretha Franklin, Chris Cornell, or Robert Plant sing, something amazing they all have in common is that they sing as if their very lives depend on it. They sing as if that day might just be the last day of their lives.

That is the energy I want you to put into your invocations. *Feel* every word, whether you are speaking it or singing it. Use that juicy emotion to send ripples of your intent out into the universe, and know that big work has just been done.

So many people think of angels as if they were celestial beings that lived far away from us in heaven or in the clouds. But really, they are right here, right now, with you all the time. So again, imagine them as if they are loving friends standing side by side with you, always ready to help you out. Especially when you are doing an invocation.

## Singing

When you're invoking your angels, you can also sing to your angels. Singing can really help raise both the energy and the emotion of what you're calling out, so over the years I've found it to be very effective. Many of the people I work with tell me they prefer to sing their invocations versus just speaking them out loud. Singing them also helps you maintain your focus and brings an extra "party" vibe into the work. And let me tell you, angels do love to see you enjoying yourself.

So, if you love getting your song on and are in the mood to sing your angels a love song, please feel free to create songs out of the invocations in this book.

## Writing Down Your Requests

Although I will be giving you an invocation for each of the 21 days, you can also create your own invocations infused with your intentions. Writing down your request is always a good idea. When you're working on something big, like manifesting more wealth or a new job, feel free to make it known. For example, you can write it out like this:

> *Dear angels,*
> *I invoke you to come into my life to bring me mas-*
> *sive amounts of wealth in all kinds of mysterious ways*
> *and to help me remove any blocks or stagnant energy*
> *that stands in my way. Thank you, dear angels.*

At the end of every invocation, it's extremely important to bring in gratitude. Make sure you give gratitude to the angels by saying thank you to them. All beings, visible or invisible, love to be buttered up, so after every magical act, remember to show gratitude to your angels for the work that they are supporting you with, even if your request hasn't quite manifested yet.

## The Master Invocation

Now that you have learned what kind of energy and attitude to bring to your invocations, let's go ahead and practice one.

I am going to give you the Master Angel Invocation, which you can do today. The Master Angel Invocation calls upon all the orders of the angels, major and minor, to come to your aid immediately. The Master Angel Invocation will give your angel magic a big boost. It is a highly effective method for getting all the angels' attention and letting them know that you are ready, willing, and able to invite them into your life right now to come to your aid in all manner of miraculous ways.

Before I give you this invocation, I want you to first contemplate an intention for the next 21 days. What do you really need help with resolving? What area of your life is screaming for some lovin'? What kind of additional support do you need? Do you need clarity in a certain area of your life?

Sit quietly with yourself and choose just one intention. Write it down.

Now go find the perfect spot for you to recite the Master Invocation aloud. Ideally, you'll want to find an area in your home or outside where you can speak freely and you won't be interrupted.

Make sure to include your personal intention at the end of the invocation. And remember to use emotion!

### The Master Invocation

*I now call on the Creator of All That Is [or whichever term you are most comfortable using, such as God/Source/Great Spirit, etc.], the angels and archangels, Thrones and Dominions, Principalities and Powers and Virtues of heaven, Cherubim and Seraphim, and especially you, my dear guardian angel. Please intercede for me and help me to see miracles in my life and bring miraculous solutions to _____ _____ [state your personal intention that you wrote down earlier].*

After reciting your invocation, how does it feel? Do you notice any shift around you or in your space now that you've done it? Do you notice feeling a deeper sense of calm or that you are more relaxed? These are the things to watch out for when doing invocations and angel work. These are signs that the angels are near.

Soon I'm going to teach you about creating a sacred space in your home and give you your 21 daily invocations that will begin inviting specific archangels into your life. But before I do that, I have to mention something that's really important for the success of your daily practice and angel magic: Invoking is only one-half of the recipe. You can be the best, most passionate invocation rockstar in the world, but it doesn't necessarily mean you're going to receive your desired result. Why is this?

The typical reasons you may not get the result you intended are (a) you haven't learned how the angels communicate back to you, and (b) you haven't learned how to see the world through a more playful, magical, and spiritual lens. So, to help you make the most of this experience, in the next section we will cover all the creative ways that angels will communicate back to you.

---- ❧ ----

# How the Angels Talk to You

People often get impatient when they begin consciously working with angels because they want a big, juicy, explosive first encounter with their angels. If you are someone who is waiting for Archangel Michael to make a 3-D appearance in your room, giant wings ablaze and angel choirs singing in the background, then you may be waiting a while. Though I am a huge fan of big and juicy angel encounters, from the years of doing this work for myself and others, I know that the angels don't always come through that way.

Patience is required when working with angels, and so is managing your expectations. Those are two big keys in allowing angel messages to come through.

So that you know what to watch for, in this chapter we will discuss the variety of cool and creative ways that the angels can break through and get their messages of love, support, and validation across to you. This next part of the book is critical to your success in manifesting miracles with the help of the angels.

It's one thing to pray to or invoke the angels, but it's a whole different thing to actually be aware of the answers they bring.

## No Coincidences

Before I teach you the different ways that angels communicate with you, there is one thought that I want you to delete from your consciousness. This thought will absolutely block you from the reality of angels and miracles, so it's important that you get rid of it once and for all.

The thought is "That was just a coincidence."

The angels are master manifesters, and when you begin talking to them, they will do everything in their power to let you know they are real and right there with you.

Your angels send you signs of love, comfort, and even protection all the time, but one of the main reasons you may not have noticed them is because you may have been telling yourself all along that every cool thing that happens to you is "just a coincidence." This one thought will suck your angel magic dry fast, so get rid of it from here on out.

Let's reimagine this whole "coincidence" nonsense together. Have you ever turned on the radio and the song that came on had a message in it that was just what you needed to hear? Have you ever had a magical solution to a problem appear out of nowhere just in the nick of time? Have you ever met someone in such a weird way that it just seemed to be kismet?

Take a moment now to think of some of the more unexplainable and magical things that have happened to you that you might have written off as coincidences. When you add them all together, they start building a picture that doesn't seem like coincidence at all. These little things can happen to you daily. They can be large or small, and if you dismiss them, you are missing the golden truth: that you are not alone. Your angels are listening to you, supporting you, and actively helping you whenever and wherever they can.

From now on, know that every so-called coincidence is actually help and support from your angels and the divine. If you master this one mental shift, your life will open up to a magical world that has been hiding from you in plain sight: the world of the miraculous.

## Subtle Angel Signs:
## Intuition and Your Intuitive Senses

Angel signs won't always look like what you might expect them to look like. Sometimes they will be big and loud, but other times they will be subtle and soft. The key to being able to recognize those signs, and to receiving the angels' love and clear guidance as a result, is to tap into your gut instincts and your subtle senses, also known as your intuition.

We all have intuition, whether we are aware of it or not. Your intuition is like a muscle, and the more you flex it, the greater it grows.

Listening to your intuition and your intuitive

senses is the most important skill you can learn in working with angels. Your intuition holds the voice of your soul, your song, and your essence. It's through your intuition, your thoughts, and your feelings that the angels pass on amazing loving guidance. I don't want you to miss this guidance, because you could be missing pure gold.

Most people in the West haven't had much practice in flexing the muscle of their subtle senses, because Western culture tends to place a much heavier emphasis on logic and linear thinking than on intuitive, heart-centered consciousness. We in the West are so used to overidentifying with our loud, tantrum-like logical mind that we often completely overlook the awesomeness that is our intuition. And when I say "awesome," I mean *awesome!*

It takes some practice, but if all you did was slow down and learn to listen to the still, small voice of your heart, instead of that wild pack of wolves in your head, life would go a lot more smoothly.

There is no better time than the present to begin learning to develop and trust your subtler senses. And they can be very, very subtle. For example, one of the reasons you might miss the subtler angel signs or messages over the next 21 days is that the intuitive messages you are receiving might seem like your own thoughts and feelings.

Ever have an epiphany or a really amazing idea that all of a sudden hits you over the head? That just might be your invisible posse, your dear angels, showering you with divine inspiration.

Ever needed to solve a problem in your life and the solution came to you out of the blue when you weren't even thinking about it? Yeah, that was your angels too.

The more you pay attention to your thoughts and feelings, the more you will become attuned to when your angels are helping you out and giving you guidance.

So make sure you pay attention to any beautiful and inspired thoughts and feelings or flashes of insight that happen for you during your angel journey. Write them down, and don't assume that those thoughts and feelings are your own, especially if they are repetitive and seem to be more hopeful, creative, and optimistic than usual. Open yourself up to the possibility that they are instead your angels leading you toward your new and amazing miraculous life.

## More Obvious Angel Signs

Over the past few years, I have been hosting a Facebook group called the 7-Day Miracle Challenge, and it's a place where angel lovers all over the world gather to share their angel experiences. People post daily about the fantastic and mind-blowing angel-related things that are happening for them.

Below, I share with you some of the more common angel signs and experiences that people report in our Facebook community and that I have also experienced along the way. Some signs are subtler than others, so I hope this list of my top 11 signs will help you recognize when your angels are trying to get your attention.

### 1. Feathers

Finding feathers on the ground or in interesting places is one of the most popular experiences that people post about in our group.

Finding any color or kind of feather is often a message or validation from the angels and Spirit. However, white feathers are classically known to represent love from the angels.

Over the next 21 days, please keep your eyes peeled for feathers along your path. They are meaningful and often come at times when you need validation or an extra dose of good juju.

After an angel workshop that I taught, one of my students went home and opened her kitchen cabinet to get a cookbook. She pulled down the cookbook, and out flew a big white feather that floated to the ground. She couldn't believe it, as we had just talked about white feathers and angel signs that afternoon. Coincidence? After that moment, she knew the angels were with her, and over the next several days she had many more such experiences.

### 2. Light

Angels are made of light, so often angels can show up and manifest as all kinds of light anomalies. Some people catch twinkles in the corner of their eye or see flashing colors when they close their eyes. Sometimes angels will even show up as orbs, rays, or streaks in photos.

Keep your eyes peeled for lights dancing in the variety of ways that they can, and trust that it's angel activity.

### 3. Signs (Literally)

Sometimes angels will communicate with you through signs such as license plates, magazines, billboards, and bumper stickers. This type of message gets reported to me all the time and is probably one of the most prominent ways that the angels communicated to me in the beginning.

Also pay special attention if you see Bible verses highlighted on license plates or anywhere else. If you see a sign that says *Psalms 91:11* or something else that might seem like a Bible verse, make sure to look it up. These are often direct communications to you by your angels. Usually the messages are exactly what you need when you need them.

It is amazing what the angels can do with all the signs that are around us, so if you happen to start seeing meaningful words or are drawn to certain cars' license plates or billboards, trust that these are true messages from your angels. They can be so spot-on and obvious that it will knock your socks off!

### 4. Nature

Nature is a powerful vehicle for angelic and divine manifestations. Angels especially love showing themselves overhead through cloud formations, rainbows, or light anomalies in the sky. In our online angel community, people post images of these beautiful sights almost daily.

Another popular way that nature and the angels conspire together to give you love is through the beautiful animals. Birds showing up at just the right time or peculiar animals showing up and looking at you in meaningful ways are often signs from the angels that you are supported and that the angels are listening.

On a side note, if you see the same kind of animal over and over again, please do an internet search on that animal. For example, if you see robins everywhere you look, search for "robin spirit animal." You just might be blown away at how the meaning of that particular animal is exactly what you need to know.

## 5. *Recurring Numbers*

A classic number that pops up regularly when working with angels is 444, but any number that appears in triples — like 111, 222, 333, etc. — can also be a sign of angel juju. Each number has different meanings, so if you see a number repeating often, google it! There are many interpretations of the significance of these numbers, so it's really up to you and your intuition to decide what makes sense for you. As with so many angel signs, you'll often be amazed at how the numbers' meanings exactly match the kind of guidance and validation you need.

## 6. People

Messages also come through other people, so pay attention. Is someone sharing with you something you were just asking the angels for help with? Did you hear someone talking on the subway about a specific topic that is somehow related to information you are asking for?

It is fascinating how the right people show up in your life and give you exactly what you need, right when you need it. The more you work with angels, the more this happens.

Children are particularly wonderful at delivering messages from the angelic realm because they are still so open — they haven't closed themselves off yet to magic or to the spirit world. They sometimes can directly channel angel messages without even knowing why they are saying what they are saying. It's quite beautiful and profound, so instead of always thinking that you are there to teach your child about life, be open to the fact that your child is also there to teach you a thing or two that goes beyond reason. The wisdom that can pour through them can be quite amazing.

## 7. Music

Angels can bring you love, comfort, and even advice over the radio waves, and they do it masterfully and with absolute divine timing. I can't count the number of times I have walked into a grocery store or an office building, and the song playing over the speakers seemed like a direct message from my angels. Many people in our community also report the incredible gifts that the angelic realm brings to them through song, in exactly the moment when they need the message most.

Over the next 21 days, open your ears. You will be surprised by how often the songs on the radio, jingles in commercials, or music piped in at the dentist's office will speak directly to you and your life circumstances.

### 8. Dreams

Angels can also make appearances in your dreams to bring you miraculous solutions. Please pay attention to your dreams. Write down your dreams every morning, and review them frequently over the next 21 days, because often there are gems hidden within dreams that are the answers to our deepest questions and prayers.

### 9. Synchronicities

Synchronicities — what many call "coincidences" — are very common when you are calling on the angels for support. It is the angels' way of showing you that you are on the right track, encouraging you to have faith and to trust in what is happening.

You are actually getting signs and synchronicities daily already, but you simply haven't been paying attention to them as much as you can. The more you do this work, the more they will pop out at you.

## *10. Social Media*

Social media platforms such as Facebook and Instagram are places where angels like to hang out and send messages, give validation, and hand out answers to questions. Ever see a quote on your feed just when you needed to hear that exact advice? Guess who sent you that message? That's right, the angels.

The angels are absolutely relentless when it comes to your social media newsfeed, so make sure to pay attention to the information that pops up there. And remember, for the next 21 days *there is no such thing as a coincidence.*

## *11. Touch*

Yes, the angels can and will touch you. This is by far my favorite kind of angel encounter. People all over the world report having goose bumps when the angels are near. We call those "angel bumps." They also can tap your shoulder, give you a little peck on the cheek, hold your hand, or give you an overarching feeling of warmth and comfort.

Working with angels will open up and activate your energy body. People often start feeling tingly electrical currents moving through their bodies when angels are near, and these tingles are often accompanied by feelings of peace, comfort, and/or joy.

So if during these 21 days you are overcome with a feeling of effervescent warmth and comfort, please know it is your angels wrapping their goodness around you to show you that they are with you.

Now that you know both the subtle and more obvious ways that angels communicate with you, next I will share some pro-tips on how you can get the most out of working with the archangels during our time together. These tips come from years of doing this work for myself and with others, so make sure to pay close attention to each tip so that you can get the most out of this miraculous journey.

# Pro-Tips for Success

Each day of the Angel Experiment was channeled by me on behalf of the angels. Every day, I sat quietly with the angels and asked them, "What gift would you like to give us today?" Day by day, the angels revealed the 21 teachings, invocations, and healing meditations that you will find in the subsequent pages.

The final product is a beautiful tapestry of love, comfort, warmth, and spiritual power all wrapped up in these 21 angel-inspired days.

For the next 21 days you will be entering a world where anything is possible. Before you get started, I want to ensure that you have everything you need to make this miraculous experiment an absolute success.

That said, please read this section of the book carefully, and do your best to follow the guidelines and best practices that I share with you in the pages to come.

I want you to invite in these magical helpers in the most powerful way possible.

## Download Your Free Audio MP3 Invocations

I have prepared 21 free MP3s for you. They are the companion guided audio meditations for each day's practice.

You may prefer guiding yourself through these healing meditations on your own. However, listening to the recorded guided meditations will help you to relax and surrender to the process even more, so I highly recommend using them. You can find them at TheAngelExperimentAudios.com.

## Get a Journal

Get a dedicated journal just for this experiment. You can use a paper journal, or you can keep a "virtual" journal via your laptop or smartphone. Use whichever feels best for you, depending on your lifestyle.

The real key here is to make sure you always have a way to document your angelic happenings quickly. They can take place at any time of the day, and you will want to have a way to capture those miraculous moments before you forget about them.

Keeping solid records of your experiences over the next 21 days is incredibly important. Human memory consistently fails over stretches of time, and many little details can easily be forgotten. This is why scientists keep impeccable records throughout the course of their experiments, and why I want you to amass accurate and consistent data over these next 21 days.

With angel work, even "little" events matter because in the end they all add up to create quite a magical and clear picture for you. There are no events too small to note, so please take note of anything and everything magical, synchronistic, or miraculous during your angel sojourn.

Here is how I recommend you format your journal entries: write down the questions below in the beginning of your journal, and answer each of these questions daily.

- How did I feel before today's invocation and meditation?
- How did I feel after today's invocation and meditation?
- Did I receive any intuitive messages or feelings during today's meditation?
- What synchronicities have happened for me today?
- Have I been seeing any recurring numbers?
- Any inspiring ideas?
- Any other signs or messages from my angels?
- Did anything good or amazing happen to me today?
- Did I notice anything that seemed like divine timing or that came right when I needed it?
- What was my overall mood for the day?

## Set Up a Sacred Space

I invite you to create a sacred space or personal altar in your home. An altar is small area inside your home that you dedicate as your special place to connect with the divine. Think of it as a beautiful home-based mini church, temple, or sacred place that's just for you, where you can commune with the angels and invite them into your life.

Over the years I have found that people deeply love creating sacred spaces and receive great healing and benefit from having them in their homes. People tell me that they receive feelings of warmth and comfort from having them, and it makes their home feel safer and more sacred.

Here is a simple list of items you can use to get started creating your sacred space:

- Altar cloth
- Silk scarves
- Inspired artwork
- Candle
- Incense
- Oracle deck
- Flowers
- Feathers
- Crystals
- Sacred pictures or figurines of angels or other divinities that you love
- Anything else that has meaning to you or that inspires you

Everything you place on your altar should have special significance to you, but it doesn't have to be big and fancy. It can be tiny and simple. Please do whatever feels right for you, and know that when you bring the sacred into even the smallest corner of your home, your home becomes sacred. Have fun with this one, and take your time creating a beautiful and welcoming space for you to convene with your angels.

One last thing on this: you do not always have to be at your sacred space to do your invocations, but you do always have to be in a place where you can find silence and stillness and where you won't be interrupted during these healing attunements with the angels.

Folks with extra-busy households often struggle to have any alone time at all. If you're one of them, feel free to get creative. Some people have used their cars or even their bathrooms (with the door locked) to carve out sacred time with their angels. If you have a fast-paced or hectic household, you may want to consider waking up 15 minutes earlier than everyone else and using that time for this sacred communication with your angels.

## Set Your Intention

Though having an intention is not required for this angel experiment, it is a good idea to have one. This will help you focus your angel magic toward a specific area in your life over the next 21 days. You already chose an intention earlier in this book when we did the Master Invocation. However, I want to give you an opportunity now to review the intention that you set and make sure that it still feels like the best choice. Does it represent the area of your life that you feel could use the biggest boost of angel juju? Remember, there is nothing off-limits when it comes to the angels, so whether you need help with a new career, your relationship, your children, your health, or your finances, please name it so that your angels can begin working their magic for you.

Choose one specific intention and write it in present tense in your journal. Here are some examples of intentions written in the present tense so that you can get the hang of it:

- I have plenty of money to pay my bills and more.
- I feel healthy, youthful, and alive.
- I feel loved deeply in all my relationships.
- I have all the time I need to get everything done and to have fun.
- I feel happy and confident in my life.
- I am successful at work and at home.

Next, you can invoke the angels to help you fully embody your intention. Here's a simple format for you to follow when writing your intention for the angels:

*Dear angels,*
*Help me know, feel, and embody the truth of*
_____ *[input your*
*request] now.*

Get the idea? Good! Now come up with your own intention, write it down, place it front and center for your angels to see (in your sacred space or another special place where you can review it regularly), and let the magic begin working for you.

## Do Every Day's Practice for
## 21 Days No Matter What!

I've found that, because our lives are often filled with responsibilities, some people have a difficult time committing to doing just about anything for 21 days straight. For this reason, I want you to make a mental shift and commit that, come hell or high water, you will meet with your angels daily for all 21 days.

If you are an extra-busy person, one thing that will help you to complete these days successfully is to schedule your meditation times in your calendar. These practices will take up only 10 to 15 minutes a day, so they shouldn't be too hard to fit into even the most hectic schedules.

Again, it's quite possible that the angels brought this book into your hands for a reason, so make sure to work this process the way that the angels intended for it to support your life.

So much wild healing and magic goes on for the people who complete this process successfully, and I want nothing more than for you to be one of them. Work these 21 days like a boss, and commit to doing them wholeheartedly.

### Do Each Day Sequentially

It may be tempting to skip ahead in the book or to trade out one day for another, but don't do that. As a matter of fact, if I were you I would make it a point *not* to look ahead in the 21 days at all. Do your best to always keep the next day a mystery.

Each day builds on the one before, and the angels placed these daily invocations and healings in this specific order for a reason. Doing them out of order or jumping around might inhibit the magic of the experiences that the angels intend for you.

## Pay Attention

Before and after each meditation, notice how you feel physically. Before you sit with the angels, pay attention to how you are breathing and whether there is any tension or pressure in your body. Another thing to notice is how you feel emotionally. Are you feeling any anxiety? Or maybe you are feeling a little blue? Compare it with how you feel after performing that day's meditation and invocation, and always make sure to record your findings in your journal.

Noticing your feelings before and after each day's practice is important so that you can become aware of the subtler changes and healing that happen for you as the days progress. The more you become aware of these shifts, the more they will multiply.

Here are some of the common experiences to watch out for during your meditations:

- Electrical currents running through parts or all of your body
- Cool breezes or body parts feeling cool
- Warmth
- Sweating
- Bloating, burping, gas
- Feeling lightness around you

- Feeling a presence with you
- A sense of peace and ease
- Tears falling down your face

The above experiences are often directly related to energy movement and the presence of angels. If things like these happen for you, don't forget to write them down in your journal!

## The Power of Nature

Woven through ancient religious texts, nature has often been the theater by which the divine has made its powerful and miraculous contact with humankind. If you look closely at the stories of the masters and prophets, many of their biggest divine encounters happened in the great outdoors. Moses talked to God via a burning bush. The Buddha sat under a bodhi tree and became enlightened. Muhammad was visited by an archangel in a cave who revealed to him the beginnings of the holy Koran. Jesus was led to the wilderness by the Holy Spirit. And the list goes on.

I'm bringing this to your attention because nature quite simply is alive with the divine. It's alive, it's listening, and it's a deep healer to the human soul. Because of this, nature is the perfect playground for you to frolic with your angels. Feel free to do some of your invocations surrounded by the beauty of nature. Take the time to go for walks or hikes over the course of this journey. The angels are always listening, and they love creating heavenly spectacles for spiritual seekers. So make sure to get outside as often as you can over the next 21 days, and of course, keep your eyes peeled for divine activity.

## How to Work with the "Downloads"

At the end of each day's meditation, I will direct you to the "Downloads" section of the practice. These downloads represent new loving thoughts or feelings that Source and the angels would like you to be connected with.

Most people don't realize this, but part of the reason why our lives are so full of struggle is because our subconscious minds are programmed with extremely negative thoughts and limiting beliefs that we inherited from our families, our ancestors, and our culture at large. I have learned over the years that through the power of the divine, a person can easily shift and reprogram these faulty beliefs and be reconnected with beautiful feelings of love, hope, abundance, and the joy that is our true nature.

As part of this adventure, the angels had me channel new thoughts and feelings that they would like to connect you with to boost your capacity to receive the love and magic that they will be throwing your way. All you have to do to receive these amazing gifts is be willing to receive them.

Here's how to properly receive the new thoughts and feelings that the angels would like to gift to you: when you get to the "Downloads" section of the day, simply read aloud each statement that you would like to be true for you, and the new thought or feeling will be instantly downloaded into the deep reaches of your consciousness with the help of your angels and Creator.

If you are using the free MP3 recordings I have provided, all you have to do simply say "Yes" aloud after I read the downloads, and those new thoughts and feelings will come to you. This will give Source and the angels all the permission they need to connect you with these new, high-vibe thoughts and feelings.

Think of these new thoughts and feelings as gifts from the universe. It will be up to you to accept them, so make sure to do this portion of your daily practice if you want an extra sprinkle of healing and support.

Now that you have read through all my juicy tips for success, it's time to get you acquainted with the archangels and other angels that will be your hosts during this 21-day adventure. Roll out the red carpet and meet these wonderful and mysterious allies.

# Introduction to the Archangels and Other Angelic Orders

Throughout human history, invisible benevolent beings known by many names have been written about in sacred texts and revered as messengers of the divine that aid humanity. Several classes of angels have been described over the millennia, and we'll focus on the nine orders of angelic beings described in Judeo-Christian texts: the Seraphim, Cherubim, Thrones, Dominions, Virtues, Powers, Principalities, archangels, and angels. Think of these nine orders as large teams of angels that execute unique duties within the universe. Our main focus during these 21 days will be on the archangels.

I didn't learn about angels through reading about them — I learned about them mostly through my own experience — but there is some value in having a basic understanding of the roles that the angels and archangels have historically played in the lives of humans. So, in this chapter, I will give you a brief overview of the archangels and a few of the other orders of angels to give you some of the common collective thoughts about these spiritual heavies.

Different sources give conflicting accounts of exactly how many angels and archangels there are. In any case, for this book, 12 archangels, plus the Seraphim, Cherubim, Virtues, and Principalities, came forward to participate in this 21-day adventure with you. These angels will be our focus.

The archangels are known as the big cheeses of the orders of the lesser angels (angels occupying a position closer to the earthly realm). They are the boss men and women of the lower angelic realm. Each works with legions of angels beneath them. You might think of archangels as vice presidents of the universe that oversee their own unique, specialized departments.

Archangels often encompass both male and female qualities, and they may appear as different genders at different times. What is true for all the archangels is that they embody and vibrate the unconditional love of Source. Working with the archangels is a profound tool to raise your vibration, increase your joy, peace, and happiness, and improve your health.

The information I have provide here is not meant to be the ultimate law about the archangels; consider it to be a light introduction to the hosts of this adventure. These are the angels that came forward, one by one, to bring you healing gifts and angel attunements.

Beyond what I have written here about the archangels and the others, remember that what is most important is that you have your own experiences with these powerful and supportive beings. Developing your own unique relationship with the angels and archangels is the highest form of knowledge, so make sure to lean heavily on the intuitive information that you receive during your journey, and less on the descriptions given by others.

The following angels will be coming forward to work with you during this miraculous angel experience. I hope you'll enjoy getting more acquainted with these divine beings during the days to come.

## Archangel Ariel: "Lion of God"

Archangel Ariel has the duty of protecting and healing nature and wild animals. She can inspire you with her lionlike qualities, which include fierceness, strength, and passion. She also governs elemental beings such as fairies and nature spirits and can help deepen your relationship with both the physical and mystical aspects of nature. She is highly magical and can help give your manifesting power a big boost. Call on her to connect you to the healing power of the earth and to help you manifest a new job, a new home, or abundance. Her central message is "You are always connected to the abundance and power of nature."

## Archangel Azrael: "Angel of God"

Archangel Azrael's primary role is to help humans cross over to the spiritual dimensions after death. He is a great comforter to those who are dying, those who have just passed the threshold, and those left behind in grief. He also helps in healing emotional and mental imbalances and illnesses. Archangel Azrael can transmute emotional suffering into a deep calm and peace through quieting and balancing the voice of the human ego. He can also help bring peaceful endings to any area of life that has grown tired, old, and outdated. His central message is "You are always connected to the spirit world through love."

## Archangel Chamuel: "He Who Sees God"

Archangel Chamuel is a conduit of unconditional love and peace in all relationships and areas of life. He is known as a high-level healer within the hierarchy of the angels, and his role is to defend humankind from fear-based energy. He can radiate warmth in the heart chakra (one of the seven main chakras, or the energy centers that run up and down the spine), which opens and heals the heart, allowing a deeper connection with and deeper love for oneself and others. He also happens to be very skilled at finding lost material items, as well as soulmates. Call on Archangel Chamuel if you are searching for anything or need more peace or true love in your life. If you are having a sleepless night, you can also call on him to bring peace to your heart and mind so that you can go back to sleep. His central message is "Love and peace flow freely to you now."

### Archangel Haniel: "Joy of God"

Archangel Haniel represents feminine nurturing energy and has a special focus on harmony and healing within familial relationships. She is the ultimate booster of true joy, a joy that comes from within, is not attached to external factors, and is deeply connected to Source. If you experience hopelessness or are searching for grace and ease in your close relationships, call on Archangel Haniel to help. Archangel Haniel is also associated with the full moon, psychic abilities, and divine magic, and because of her deep, watery nature, she can help you boost your intuition and spiritual gifts. Her central message is "Divine joy is always within."

### Archangel Metatron: "One Who Guards"

Archangel Metatron is believed to once have been a human and is said to have brought writing and books to humankind. He helps with clearing negative thought patterns and replacing them with positive ones. He often is seen using a tool called "Metatron's cube," which is made up of all the sacred shapes of the universe and can rid people of unwanted energies. He guides us to use our spiritual power for good, to help humanity sustain itself. He is also the recorder of all our life choices.

Metatron holds the blueprint of all creation, acts as the bridge between humanity and the divine, and creates and maintains all sacred geometry. He also helps children, especially those who are sensitive and spiritually gifted. His main message is "Your divine power is always available to you."

## Archangel Michael: "He Who Is Like God"

Archangel Michael, the warrior, is a fierce protector who helps with guidance on our life purpose. He can powerfully clear negative emotions and fear-based energy. He has been mentioned in the Bible, the Torah, and the Koran. The most famous legend of Archangel Michael is that he defeated Satan. He is the archangel to call on if you feel you need protection or help confronting your inner demons, anxieties, fear-based entities, or anything that means you harm. His main tool is his magnificent sword of light, as well as his army of angels, a.k.a. his Band of Mercy. He is a master cord cutter and clearer of all energy that leads to a feeling of separation from Source. His main message is "You are eternally safe."

## Archangel Raguel: "Friend of God"

Archangel Raguel works to bring peace, cooperation, and harmony to relationships of all kinds on earth as well as in heaven. Any sort of misunderstanding or conflict can be divinely mediated by Raguel's healing vibration. His duty is to resolve discord and restore order and harmony that is aligned with the best outcome and highest good of all. He also oversees the collective service of the archangels to ensure synchronized efforts and maximized benefit for the good of humankind. Lastly, Archangel Raguel manages the earthly manifestation of events connected to our soul contracts. His central message is "Harmony is available to you in each moment."

## Archangel Raphael: "One Who Heals"

Archangel Raphael harnesses divine healing energy to heal the physical, emotional, and spiritual realms in humans and all other animals, often using an emerald-green light. Raphael is holder of the DNA keys and can work directly with our DNA to bring greater health. He also has the power to call in the love that we need in our lives to heal, whether it be through partnerships, friendships, or work relationships. He can heal humans at the soul level, erase karmic debts, and heal addictions. His main message is "Healing is possible."

## Archangel Raziel: "Secrets of God"

Archangel Raziel acts as the gatekeeper to the mysteries of the universe. He reigns over all things mystical, mysterious, and metaphysical. Dreams, psychic development, and communication between the material and spiritual worlds are his areas of expertise. He can help you use all your senses to experience divine guidance. He governs the veil between the earthly and spiritual planes. Call on Archangel Raziel when you want to gain deep spiritual understanding, boost your magic and psychic abilities, or find unexpected miracles. His central message is "Divine magic is real."

## Archangel Sandalphon: "Co-worker"

Archangel Sandalphon's role is to deliver and prioritize our prayers. He is quite good at opening our hearts and revealing all we have to be grateful for in our lives. He also heals through music on earth and brings beautiful harmonies from heaven, and he can manifest messages from Spirit that come in the form of things you hear but that are inaudible to others, known as clairaudient communications. He is the archangel to call on when you are looking for help with writing or creating music. He was once a human, along with Archangel Metatron. Archangel Sandalphon determines the best way for our prayers to be answered, based on our soul's destiny. His central message is twofold: "Music is a balm for the soul, and your prayers are always received."

## Archangel Uriel: "Light of God"

Archangel Uriel reigns in the intellectual realm, and his guidance comes to us through our thoughts, insights, and creative solutions. He is the one to call on when we are seeking epiphanies and divine inspiration. He uses his powerful light to illuminate our perception and reveal the answers we need. His gifts to us are clarity, insight, and divine understanding. He can provide prophetic warnings and information, and he also watches over recovery from natural disasters. His central message is "Your mind connects you to the divine."

### Archangel Zadkiel: "The Righteousness of God"

Archangel Zadkiel helps facilitate forgiveness, compassion, and divine mercy toward ourselves and others. He is the angel to call on when we feel stuck in the throes of unforgiveness or harsh judgments. He also helps heal victims of abuse. Archangel Zadkiel can offer a deep soul cleansing in the service of finding your soul's path, work/life balance, and forgiveness. He also is a guide and healer for all issues related to sexuality. His central message is "Forgiveness is divine freedom."

### Order of the Cherubim

Perhaps you have seen or heard of cherubs, maybe in relation to Valentine's Day or in medieval paintings? They are the beautiful beings that create the order of the Cherubim. These angels are often seen and depicted as winged children, and they are the attendants to God. The Cherubim embody qualities such as innocence, childlikeness, and playfulness and have been seen historically as angels of love. They help lift the hearts of humans and are symbols of redeemed humanity, or humanity in its perfected and most innocent form.

### Order of the Principalities

This order of angels is known to support and express the divine will. They're like middle management that govern the lower orders of angels. They also work very closely with humankind to support us and God in executing the divine plan. They support humans in following the path of joy and help awaken the divine mission and service within each soul.

## Order of the Seraphim

These angels are described as having six wings each and are considered the highest order of angels, the angels closest to God. When connected with intuitively, the Seraphim often appear to be fiery, radiant beings whose light can fill up the room. They are imbued with the "fire of God" and help humans ignite their own fire for the divine within them.

## Order of the Virtues

This order of the angels works closely with humans to support miracles and manifestation. The Virtues carry immense divine strength and are known to help humans strengthen and deepen their faith in Source/God/Creator.

Now that you have been acquainted with the angels who will be assisting you in this adventure, I want you to take a brief moment to say hello to them right now. Close your eyes, center yourself, and imagine that all the angels mentioned in this chapter are standing around you. Let them know that you are ready to let go of your outdated, tired old beliefs about yourself and your life and that you are ready for miracles.

## Ready, Set, Go!

You have everything you need to start this journey off strong, so you're now officially ready to kick off this angel goodness with a bang!

In the next part of this book, you will find all the invocations and meditations for each of the 21 days ready for you. Prepare yourself for some deep angel lovin'. Have fun with this, keep an open mind, and get ready to throw down a serious party with your angels.

Ready, set, go!

# PART II

---- ❖ ----

# YOUR 21-DAY
## ANGEL
# EXPERIMENT

---- ❖ ----

# DAY 1

------ ❧ ------

# Miracles

## *with Archangel Michael and Archangel Metatron*

Today's invocation and meditation will attune you to the vibration of miracles.

Miracles come in many sizes, large and small. Some are obvious, while others can be subtle. Not only will this invocation help you dissolve some of the energetic blocks that are preventing you from fully witnessing and experiencing miracles, but it will also open your awareness to all the surprising ways that miracles can show up in your life.

Today, Archangel Michael and Archangel Metatron will be invoked to clear and attune your body, heart, and mind to the energetic field of miracles.

When you are ready to begin, find a quiet spot, center yourself, and recite this invocation aloud:

❧ *Day 1 Invocation*

> *Dear Creator of All That Is, Archangel Michael, Archangel Metatron, and all the holy orders of the angels,*

*I open myself up to you now, today, to receive all the miracles that my life has to offer me. I believe in miracles, and I ask that any blocks that stand in the way of my truly experiencing miracles be dissolved and transformed into the highest light.*

*I thank you so much for all your help, dear angels.*

Next, either you can listen to the free guided meditation audio that I have provided to you for Day 1 or you can perform the following meditation on your own.

> *Audio meditation available at TheAngelExperimentAudios.com/Day1*

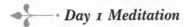 ## *Day 1 Meditation*

*Close your eyes, relax your breathing and your body, and bring your attention to the point right at the top-center of your head, also known as the crown chakra. Imagine that Archangel Michael and Archangel Metatron are standing in the room with you, right by your side, and they begin clearing out emotional or energetic toxins, anything that you do not need and are willing to release today to open you up more to miracles. Remember to take deep breaths*

*frequently, as negative energy moves through your breath out of your body and energy system.*

*Your only job is to sit and witness the angels clearing out the gunk that is blocking you from seeing a full expression of miracles in your life. As these two archangels lift any heaviness or blocks from you, I want you to imagine that they are also filling you up with the energy of miracles through the top of your head and infusing your whole body.*

*Imagine what color (or colors) make up the energy of miracles. Witness your body getting filled with that color. Allow that color to fill your whole body and all the cells of your body. Next, expand the color from your body to the space around your body and then out into the room or environment you're in. Watch that energy move through your home, your work environment, your vehicles, and everywhere you go on a daily basis. Allow your whole world to be infused with the energy of miracles.*

When you are done witnessing your whole space fill up with this beautiful energy of miracles, stay in a meditative, relaxed state while you move on to the downloads portion of this healing below. Read the downloads, with the understanding that as you do, the angels and the Creator are giving them to you instantaneously. Only read aloud the ones that really speak to you — those that represent new thoughts and feelings that you would like the angels to gift to you.

## ✂—— • *Day 1 Downloads*

- Miracles are real.
- I know how to be a powerful witness of miracles in my life.
- I am a conduit for miracles.
- I believe in miracles.
- I'm worthy of receiving miracles in my life.
- I know how to receive miracles in my life.
- I am a miracle.

After you are done reading these statements aloud, thank your angels, guides, Archangel Michael, and Archangel Metatron for suffusing the energy of miracles into your life, into your body, into your heart, into your mind, and into the world around you. Then bring your awareness back fully into the room.

Today, ask for miracles to multiply in your life so that you can see them, feel them, and experience them at the perfect pace for you. Invite miracles to come to you in all the vivacious and delicious forms that they can take. You can say today's invocation and practice its meditation as much as you want throughout the day.

Keep your eyes peeled for miracles all around you, and please remember to write down your experiences.

Angel juju coming at you.

# DAY 2

———————— ✣ ————————

# Divine Understanding

## *with Archangel Uriel and Archangel Raziel*

Today, the angels want to open your mind to the experience of divine understanding. This invocation is extremely important because you can experience all the miracles, signs, and synchronicities you want, but if you don't understand what they mean, you will not recognize the deeper significance of these events.

This 21-day angel adventure will, in fact, take your spiritual understanding to an entirely new level. Today, Archangel Uriel and Archangel Raziel would like to give you the gift of gaining profound spiritual insights, including how to pay attention to and discern the signs that you'll be seeing.

Don't you want to know why you found the feather or why you're seeing the same number over and over again? Today's healing will help you discern that information and receive it with flow and ease.

When you are ready to begin, find a quiet spot, center yourself, and recite this invocation aloud:

### Day 2 Invocation

*Dear Creator of All That Is, Archangel Uriel, and Archangel Raziel,*

*I ask you now for your help today in breaking down my limited thinking and illusions so that I can clearly understand and trust the divine guidance and signs that I'm seeing from my angels. I also ask that you open my understanding of spiritual truth and lift it to the highest possible level for me at this time. Thank you so much, Creator, Archangel Uriel, Archangel Raziel, and all the other helpers.*

Next, either you can listen to the free guided meditation audio that I have provided to you for Day 2 or you can perform the following meditation on your own.

*Audio meditation available at TheAngelExperimentAudios.com/Day2*

### Day 2 Meditation

*Place your awareness at the top of your head and imagine that Archangel Uriel and Archangel Raziel are right there with you and helping you attune to divine understanding.*

*Breathe deeply. As you do, imagine with every exhale that you're letting go of the limiting beliefs or fears that are blocking you from your true, divine genius. Witness this release intuitively as it happens. Imagine that beautiful energy from above enters through the top of your head and permeates all parts of your brain and nervous system. As it does, imagine that little points of light begin twinkling throughout your body.*

When you feel like everything inside you is all lit up and you are done with the meditation, stay sitting quietly, and read the following downloads. Only read aloud the ones that really speak to you — those that represent new thoughts and feelings that you would like the angels to gift to you.

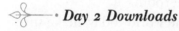

### Day 2 Downloads

- I know what it feels like to trust intuitive insights that I receive.
- I know how to read the symbolic language of the divine.
- I know what it feels like to know the truth instantly.
- I know what it feels like to interpret angel signs instantly.
- I know how to be a conduit for divine inspiration and spiritual understanding with flow and ease.
- I know what it feels like to be a genius.
- I am a genius.

- I know what it feels like to live without confusion and to have clarity in my life.
- I know how to live with clarity.
- I know how to embrace clarity.
- Clarity is mine.
- Everywhere I look, I see the signs of the divine and I understand them.
- I know what it feels like to have an understanding that defies logic, that defies space and time.
- I know how to allow my divine wisdom, my divine genius, to flow through me easily.

After you are done stating and receiving these new thoughts and feelings, thank your guides and angels. Thank Archangel Uriel and Archangel Raziel for the many blessings coming to you today. Then bring your awareness fully back into the room.

When you go out into the world today, make sure to look for flashes of insight, inspiration, and understanding. When you notice these things happening for you, make sure to write them down.

Angel juju coming at you.

# DAY 3

_____ ❧ _____

# Divine Vision and Voice

### _with Archangel Zadkiel_
### _and Archangel Raziel_

Today's invocation is designed to open up your spiritual gifts or your intuitive senses. We are all born with spiritual and intuitive abilities such as clairvoyance, which is clear seeing, and clairaudience, which is clear hearing; however, most of us are unaware of them. The reason why so many of us are unaware of our gifts is that over the years our gifts have shut down from underuse or fear.

Many people have unconscious fears blocking them from fully experiencing the beauty of these wonderful gifts, because people with awakened intuition have historically been shamed, demonized, dismissed, and even killed for having these gifts. This is deeply unfortunate, because awakening your spiritual gifts is of utmost importance if you want to fully experience the presence, power, and love of the divine in your life.

In working with my clients and teaching intuitive courses over the years, I have found that these fears

are the biggest blocks that prevent humans from seeing and hearing the divine in our daily lives.

Today's healing meditation will be the perfect opportunity for you to release the fear that is standing
in the way of your full intuitive potential. Archangels
Zadkiel and Raziel will be helping you clear out what
is blocking you from seeing and hearing the divine in
your life, and they can't wait to get started.

When you are ready to begin, find a quiet spot,
center yourself, and recite this invocation aloud:

### ᴥ⟶ Day 3 Invocation

> *Dear Creator of All That Is, Archangel Raziel, and
> Archangel Zadkiel,*
>
> *I invite you now into my life to help me clearly
> see and hear the divine in all aspects of my life. I ask
> you to remove any blocks or fears, from this lifetime or
> any previous lifetimes, that prevent me from fully see-
> ing and hearing the powerful presence of the divine.
> Thank you, Archangels Raziel and Zadkiel.*

Next, either you can listen to the free guided meditation
audio that I have provided to you for Day 3 or you can
perform the following meditation on your own.

*Audio meditation
available at
TheAngelExperimentAudios.com/Day3*

### ⚘ Day 3 Meditation

*Put all your awareness into your eyes and ears. Imagine that Archangels Raziel and Zadkiel come into the room and stand right there with you. Feel them working on opening up your eyes and your ears, clearing out any old debris, any old fear or blocks from this lifetime or previous lifetimes. Begin to feel how your divine ears and your divine eyes are more fully awakened. Breathe and imagine shadows being pulled from your head, from your eyes, from your ears, and sent up to the light.*

*Once you feel like the archangels have removed all the gunk from your eyes and ears, imagine that each of them fills your eyes and ears with beautiful light. Sometimes people see indigo or rainbow colors related to either of these archangels.*

When you feel like your eyes and ears are filled with this light and the work feels complete, then it's time to move on to the downloads portion of this attunement. Stay sitting quietly, and read the following downloads. Only read aloud the ones that really speak to you — those that represent new thoughts and feelings that you would like the angels to gift to you.

### ✂ Day 3 Downloads

- I see the signs of the divine clearly.
- It's safe for me to see visions of the divine.

- It's safe for me to hear the presence of the divine in my life.
- I know how to see and hear the presence of the divine.
- I know how to hear and see angels.
- I know what it feels like to hear and see angels daily in my life.
- I know how to easily see past the surface of all things.
- I know how to see the truth behind all things.
- I know how to see and hear divinity in all its forms.
- I know how to see and hear the power of my own divinity in all things.

With these new thoughts and feelings that you have just received from these beautiful archangels, you have now essentially received a new set of eyes and ears. Yes! Make sure to thank dear Archangels Raziel and Zadkiel for today's beautiful attunement. Then bring your awareness back into the room.

Today, pay close attention to new beautiful visions or new beautiful sounds that you notice in the world. Watch the colors and notice if they are any brighter. Make sure to write down anything that you notice today that's even just a little bit extraordinary.

Angel juju coming at you.

# DAY 4

❧

# Divine Presence
## *with Archangel Raguel*

Today is an attunement of divine presence with the
help of Archangel Raguel. One of the most beautiful
gifts that I have ever received from the angels is the
ability to actually feel them with me. I had no idea
that this was possible until it spontaneously happened
for me. It's an incredible feeling, and I'm excited the
angels want to share this experience with you.

Divine presence can show up for you in a few different ways. Sometimes it can come to you as a sense of
peace, warmth, lightness, or what I call "angel bumps"
(they feel like goose bumps with a sprinkle of joy).
Sometimes you can even feel the angels touching or
holding your hand, touching your shoulders, or even
hugging you.

Being able to feel the presence of the divine with
you lifts your vibration up to a whole new level. Your
intuitive ability of clairsentience, or clear feeling, also
gets a big boost when you are able to notice the subtle

or sometimes dramatic signs that you are in the presence of angels.

Today, Archangel Raguel will be boosting your awareness and clearing the pathways for you to be able to more easily feel and experience the presence of the divine. It's mind-blowing when it happens, and I really want it to happen for you!

When you are ready to begin, find a quiet spot, center yourself, and recite this invocation aloud:

### Day 4 Invocation

*Dear Creator of All That Is, Archangel Raguel, and all the divine orders of angels,*

*I ask you now to come to me and open up every cell of my body to your divine presence. Please help me to feel the unconditional love of creation in all areas of my body and in every cell, so that I will know once and for all that you are truly with me today and always. I thank you from the bottom of my heart for this gift and blessing, Archangel Raguel.*

Next, either you can listen to the free guided meditation audio that I have provided to you for Day 4 or you can perform the following meditation on your own.

*Audio meditation available at TheAngelExperimentAudios.com/Day4*

### Day 4 Meditation

*With your eyes closed, center yourself in your heart space and imagine Archangel Raguel coming to you and filling up your body and the bubble around your body (your aura) with pale blue light.*

*Allow this energy to flow into your body, and imagine, sense, or feel every cell in your body lighting up with this color. Watch as this energy lights up your whole being with the divine presence and energy that Archangel Raguel is sharing with you. Make sure that this light fills every cell and all the space inside you, removing and clearing any debris that prevented your ability to actually feel the divine. If you struggle to visualize this, just know and have faith that it is happening. Remember to breathe deeply every so often to support this clearing, and notice any sensations in your body as this work is done.*

When you are done with the visualization, stay sitting quietly, and read the following downloads. Only read aloud the ones that really speak to you — those that represent new thoughts and feelings that you would like the angels to gift to you.

### Day 4 Downloads

• Every cell of my body knows how to open up to the presence of unconditional love and the divine.

- I know what it feels like to really know and feel that my angels are with me.
- It is safe to feel angels.
- My body is awake to the presence of angels.
- I am worthy of feeling the presence of angels and the divine in my life.
- My body knows how to feel the presence of angels and the divine in my life.
- I love feeling the love of my angels.
- I can now feel my angels with me at all times.

After you are done with the downloads, continue to notice any shifts or changes that have happened in your body, and thank Archangel Raguel for this attunement.

Today, throughout your day, pay special attention to your body. You may feel more sensitive to touch and the sensual side of life as your body opens up to these new frequencies of love. Make sure to write down any feelings or sensations that you notice happening for you. Bring on the divine body goodness!

Angel juju coming at you.

# DAY 5

------------- ✤ -------------

# Releasing Worry
## *with Archangel Michael*

Today, we kick off three days of surrender. Learning to surrender challenging aspects of your life to a higher power is essential to living with flow and ease. Over these next three days you will learn to surrender to the angels specific heavy emotions and feelings that could be weighing down your heart and blocking you from receiving divine awesomeness.

These next three days will be a powerful detox for you so that you can step into true peace in your life. Surrendering your emotional burdens to a higher power is a wonderful way to free yourself from the baggage that you have been lugging around either consciously or unconsciously.

Today, we start with surrendering your worry to Archangel Michael. He and the other angels want you to know that they aren't here to carry away just *some* of your worry — they want to take *all* your worry from you. Yes, the angels are absolutely capable of helping you dissolve your worry and insulating you from even the most troubling aspects of your life.

Most people carry around large doses of unnecessary emotional weight, and often they don't even know it because over time they just get used to it. Well, that's not okay with me or Archangel Michael, so let's get started. Make way for Archangel Michael to help you surrender your worries and lift them up to the light.

When you are ready to begin, find a quiet spot, center yourself, and recite this invocation aloud:

### Day 5 Invocation

*Today, I call on the highest light and love, the Creator of All That Is, Archangel Michael, and his Band of Mercy to come into my heart, into my mind, into my body, and to lift all my fears and worries from me now, so that I may know true peace in my heart and in my life. Thank you, Creator, Archangel Michael, and dear, beautiful angels.*

Next, either you can listen to the free guided meditation audio that I have provided to you for Day 5 or you can perform the following meditation on your own.

*Audio meditation available at TheAngelExperimentAudios.com/Day5*

## ❖—• *Day 5 Meditation*

*Imagine Archangel Michael with his mighty sword and all his angelic helpers standing around you. Feel them beginning to lift burden after burden from you.*

*As the angels do their work, know, sense, or feel that they are lifting any fear or worry that you are storing or carrying in your belly, in your heart, or on your back. Allow this beautiful, loving, and powerful energy into your space and into every cell of your body. Use deep breaths to release your deepest worries from every cell of your body into the powerful yet loving hands of Archangel Michael.*

*If you have any particular things you've been worrying about, state them aloud to Archangel Michael. Feel free to say, "Please take this worry away from me. I don't want it anymore. I release my worries in exchange for peace. I thank you."*

*As these burdens lift from you, notice any changes in your body. You may notice lightness or tingling or changes in temperature. Whatever you notice, just observe it and continue to breathe deeply. Next, imagine that the angels are sending down vibrations of peace and of mercy, and breathe them all in. Feel yourself getting filled up with all this goodness.*

When you are done with the meditation, stay sitting quietly, and read the following downloads. Only read aloud the ones that really speak to you — those that represent new thoughts and feelings that you would like the angels to gift to you.

## Day 5 Downloads

- I know how to give my worries away to the light.
- I know it is safe to let go of my worries.
- I know things are going to carry on in my life without me worrying.
- My life flows with ease and grace.
- I am safe eternally, and my family is safe eternally.
- Everything works out for me. The universe is on my side.
- All is well for me now and forever.
- I know what it feels like to know that all is well for me now and forever.

When you are done with the downloads, thank Archangel Michael and his Band of Mercy for lifting away your worries and fear and filling you up with so much goodness.

If any worries come up throughout the day, know that Archangel Michael is right there with you to take that worry away. Imagine him standing by your side all day long, and if you feel worry bubble up, make sure to hand it on over to him.

Take special notice of your emotions today. Do you notice feeling calmer than usual? Make sure to write everything down!

Angel juju coming at you.

—————— ❧ ——————

# Releasing Grief
## *with Archangel Azrael*

On this second day of surrender, you will be letting go of grief from your heart, mind, and body with the help of Archangel Azrael.

One of the pitfalls of being human is that the amount of loss that we can experience in just one lifetime can be overwhelming. Often, we bury grief deep inside ourselves in order to survive. However, if we don't properly process or release this grief, it can take a serious toll on our mental, emotional, and even physical health. You may not even know how much grief you are storing inside you until you let go of it.

Today's powerful healing will allow you to lift out the old grief that you've been carrying around inside, so that you can feel lighter and brighter and literally breathe better. Often grief is carried in your lungs, so if you have any lung conditions, such as asthma or COPD, you may notice a big difference after today.

Get ready for Archangel Azrael to step in to lighten

your load and bring you a peaceful heart, mind, and soul.

When you are ready to begin, find a quiet spot, center yourself, and recite this invocation aloud:

### Day 6 Invocation

*Today, dear Creator, I call on Archangel Azrael to come into my body, into my mind, into my heart and lungs to release me from the deep-seated feelings of grief that are within me, in exchange for profound peace. I surrender this grief to you now. And I ask that my heart be opened to the truth of eternal life and love. Thank you, Creator, Archangel Azrael, and all the heavenly helpers, for relieving me of these burdens of grief.*

Next, either you can listen to the free guided meditation audio that I have provided to you for Day 6 or you can perform the following meditation on your own.

*Audio meditation available at TheAngelExperimentAudios.com/Day6*

### Day 6 Meditation

*Imagine Archangel Azrael coming to your side and sending a beautiful white, luminous light that begins to fill your heart and your lungs. Imagine opening your heart and your body to this light, and watch as any old grief begins to melt away. Feel yourself surrender your grief, even if you are not consciously aware of storing grief inside you.*

*You can say out loud or in your mind, "I surrender all my grief now to you, Archangel Azrael."*

*Witness and feel this beautiful energy come to you to relieve you and dissolve any grief that is ready to leave you. As the grief dissolves, imagine that Azrael's beautiful light is filling your heart, your lungs, and any other area of your body that needs this healing. Feel these areas fill up with love, light, and eternal peace.*

When this feels complete, read the following downloads. Only read aloud the ones that really speak to you — those that represent new thoughts and feelings that you would like the angels to gift to you.

### ✂ • *Day 6 Downloads*

- I know that my loved ones who have passed away, both human and animal, are safe.
- I know how to and what it feels like to love my departed loved ones without carrying grief.
- I know what it feels like to surrender all my grief to the light right now.
- I know how to and what it feels like to live without excessive grief.

- I know how to grieve, when to grieve, and when to stop grieving.
- It is safe to stop grieving.
- I know how to breathe.
- I know how to take in the breath of life, and I know what it feels like to be fully at peace.

As these beautiful new thoughts and feelings come to you and sink into your heart, mind, and body, feel Archangel Azrael's light fill the space around you. Imagine that this light is a pure, infinite source of peace and eternal love. Know that you, your family, your loved ones, and even those who have passed on are eternally safe.

Practice this meditation as often as you need to today to help soothe your soul and brighten your spirit.

Today, look for any messages that you might be receiving from your loved ones in heaven, so that they can show you that you are truly loved, that they are good and well, and that they are watching over you. And as usual, make sure to document any happenings that stand out to you.

Angel juju coming at you.

# DAY 7

❧

# Surrendering Shame
## *with All the Archangels*

Today, the third and last day of the gift of surrender, will be your chance to surrender to the archangels not just guilt but also shame. I know it sounds like a doozy, and that's because it is. Shame is a sneaky, ugly little beast that prevents us from living in our truth. It stops us from loving ourselves and feeling worthy of the love of others and the love of all that is. Along with worry and grief, many of us carry shame and don't even realize it because it's simply become an emotion that we are used to moving around in the world with. Most of us learned to be ashamed of ourselves as young children because of the messages we received from our families, friends, and cultures. Strangely, some of the things that we learned to be most ashamed about are actually our biggest gifts and what make us unique.

The angels would like to remedy this for you. Your uniqueness is your gift to the world.

When I asked which archangels would like to come

and help you lift out the deep guilt and deep shame that are encoded in all of us, guess who showed up? Not just one or two archangels, but every single one of them wanted to come and play with you today, which is incredible! Apparently, today is a big day, and the angels are ready to get to work for you. Take your time with this one, and do it as often as you get a chance today.

A special note about today is that the clearings and the downloads you will be getting are going to sound straight-up biblical, with all the sin talk. Over the years, I have found that many of us have unconscious religious beliefs that we have inherited from our culture and from our ancestry. Most of us carry beliefs like "I am a sinner" and never know it because we aren't "officially" religious. Just because you aren't religious doesn't mean that feelings like this aren't there. So in case you are carrying some of this madness around inside yourself, the angels want to help you clear it out from all levels of your being. Score for you.

When you are ready to begin, find a quiet spot, center yourself, and recite this invocation aloud:

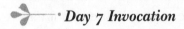 *Day 7 Invocation*

*Dear all archangels,*

*I ask that you come to me today to help me sur-render the guilt and shame that I feel deep within. Help me surrender this pain so that I may know true mercy and grace in the deepest parts of my mind, body, and soul.*

Next, either you can listen to the free guided meditation audio that I have provided to you for Day 7 or you can perform the following meditation on your own.

*Audio meditation
available at
TheAngelExperimentAudios.com/Day7*

### *Day 7 Meditation*

*Imagine a room packed full of archangels surrounding you. As you breathe, know that they are there with you. Find those areas of your body that feel tight and heavy and seem to need the most relief, and surrender all of that to the archangels.*

*Whether or not you're conscious of the guilt or shame you're carrying, it doesn't matter. Know that it is there, and willingly give it up to these divine beings. Know that it is safe to give away your guilt and shame now.*

When you are done with the meditation, stay sitting quietly, and read the following downloads. Only read aloud the ones that really speak to you — those that represent new thoughts and feelings that you would like the angels to gift to you.

## ✂ • *Day 7 Downloads*

- I release any and all beliefs that I am a sinner, I am evil, I am a bad person, and my body is sinful.
- I know what it feels like to live without the original sin.
- I know what it feels like to be absolved of my sins.
- I know what it feels like to live without being judged or without judging myself.
- I know how to, when to, and what it feels like to fully accept all of me.
- I know how to and what it feels like to forgive myself.
- I know that I'm forgiven, and I know what it feels like to be forgiven.
- I am loved.
- God/Creator forgives me.
- I know what it feels like and how to live without being ashamed of myself.
- I know how to and what it feels like to live without feeling guilty.
- I am ready to receive true mercy, and I know what it feels like to receive mercy in every cell of my being and every level of my mind now.
- I love my uniqueness.
- I now lovingly embrace all that I am.

Breathe in these new thoughts and feelings as they come to you. Open yourself up to true mercy. Know that you truly are forgiven. Allow yourself to see yourself in the perfection that the archangels see you in, like a beautiful, innocent child. Thank the archangels for this healing, and bring your awareness fully back into the room.

Today, allow yourself to imagine that you are perfect just the way you are. Let yourself feel the acceptance and love flow toward you from Spirit. You don't have to be anything else except exactly who you are, so if you catch yourself judging yourself, let that judgment go, and give it to your angels.

May today's healing blessings multiply for you every day of your life from now on. Have fun today, and, yes, write down any shifts that happen for you.

Angel juju coming at you.

——————— ⚜ ———————

# True Peace

## *with Archangel Chamuel*

Today, you are invited to receive a magic elixir that will solve all your problems. Now that you have surrendered so many of your burdens to the angels, you are ready to receive an attunement of true peace. It will be much easier for you to feel and perceive the frequency of peace after these last three days, since often the heaviness of worry, grief, shame, and guilt altogether blocks your ability to experience peace.

I have a channeled message from Archangel Chamuel for you:

*Dear Child of Love,*

*Peace is at the center of all that you are. Peace is your birthright. Please accept this gift from me today with an open heart. Allow yourself to drink in this elixir as it's truly time for peace — peace in your heart, peace in your mind, peace in your body. Say yes to peace today, and watch how quickly conflict in your outer life becomes resolved. Peace is truly who you are. Peace, peace, and peace. No more conflict, just peace.*

Thank you, Archangel Chamuel!

When you are ready to begin, find a quiet spot, center yourself, and recite this invocation aloud:

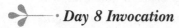 *Day 8 Invocation*

*Dear Creator and Archangel Chamuel, the archangel of peace,*

*I call upon you now to come into my heart, my mind, and my life today and radiate the energy of peace deep within me and throughout my world. I ask that any energy that stands between me and true peace be transformed to its highest vibration so that I may know true peace in the deepest layers of my heart and soul. I thank you, Creator and Archangel Chamuel, for bringing me the energy of peace in all its forms today.*

Next, either you can listen to the free guided meditation audio that I have provided to you for Day 8 or you can perform the following meditation on your own.

*Audio meditation available at TheAngelExperimentAudios.com/Day8*

## · Day 8 Meditation

*Imagine Archangel Chamuel coming into your space and bringing with him beautiful white doves that are flying around him. Imagine he places one hand over your forehead.*

*As he holds his hand there, allow him to take away anything that stands between you and true peace. Remember to keep breathing as you imagine his gentle, loving hand in front of your forehead, gently swirling around and pulling away anything that doesn't serve you at this time.*

*As he takes away these blockages, he infuses you with the energy of peace. Allow yourself to perceive what color peace represents for you.*

*Next, imagine the energy of peace flowing into your forehead, into your third eye, and cascading down your body, down to your toes, and filling up your body, slowly and gently. Allow this beautiful energy to radiate throughout every cell of your body.*

When you are done with the meditation, stay sitting quietly, and read the following downloads. Only read aloud the ones that really speak to you — those that represent new thoughts and feelings that you would like the angels to gift to you.

## · Day 8 Downloads

- True peace lives within me now.
- I am true peace.

- I know how to and what it feels like to live with true inner peace.
- I know how to radiate true peace in my home, in my work, in my relationships, and into the world.

Notice any shifts that happen in your body and your mind. Imagine Chamuel's hand still at your forehead, then envision him pulling it away, leaving a dove-shaped imprint of light right in the middle of your forehead. It will stay with you today, helping you instill your entire life with the energy of peace. Thank Archangel Chamuel, the Creator, and all the helpers who have come here today to show you that true peace is available to you.

Enjoy your day today, and look for the signs of peace all around you. Notice if you feel more peaceful toward your life circumstances throughout the day, and please do write everything down.

Angel juju coming at you.

# DAY 9

————— ✢ —————

# Purity

## *with Archangel Uriel and Archangel Zadkiel*

Today's healing is the gift of purity with Archangels Uriel and Zadkiel. Just to be clear, when I'm talking about purity, I'm not talking about chastity. I would never do that to you. We will leave chastity to the monks and nuns. For our purposes, the kind of purity that the angels are addressing here is the purity of your heart, your mind, and your soul.

Today's attunement will gently wash away the negativity, the darkness, the toxins, and the other impurities that you are carrying around within you at a soul level. Through this work, you will be put in direct and conscious contact with the purity and innocence of your own deepest and divine nature.

Here is a channeled message from Archangels Uriel and Zadkiel:

> *Dear Child of Light,*
> *Remember who you are and the purity of the essence that is your true source. All else is lies. Today,*

*ask us to remove the deep impurities in your heart,
mind, and soul in exchange for the crystal-clear purity of your own divine nature.*

Thank you, Archangels Uriel and Zadkiel!

As you prepare for today's great attunement, consider it a deep spiritual cleansing. Know that what you
experience today may or may not be subtle, but it will
be deep.

When you are ready to begin, find a quiet spot,
center yourself, and recite this invocation aloud:

### Day 9 Invocation

*Dear Creator of All That Is, Archangel Uriel, and
Archangel Zadkiel,*

*I ask you to come to me today to relieve me of the
toxins and impurities that lie deep in my heart, my
mind, and my soul that prevent me from knowing
the purity of my own divine essence. Please purify all
of me, from all places throughout space and time, so
that I may be lifted to the purest form of all that I am.
I also ask for your help in aligning all my thoughts
and actions with all that I am, today and always. I
thank you, Creator, Archangel Uriel, and Archangel
Zadkiel, for this wonderful blessing.*

Next, either you can listen to the free guided meditation audio that I have provided to you for Day 9 or you
can perform the following meditation on your own.

*Audio meditation
available at
TheAngelExperimentAudios.com/Day9*

## Day 9 Meditation

*Imagine that there is a bubble around your body.
That is your aura, the energetic field of your heart.
Then around your aura, there's an even bigger bubble that takes up even more of the room or space you're
in. Then around that bubble, there's an even bigger
bubble that might take up the whole building you're
sitting in. These bubbles represent the energetic fields
of your heart, mind, and soul.*

*Envision Archangels Zadkiel and Uriel com-
ing to you like heavenly firefighters. Imagine them
clearing you and purifying you with celestial waters.
Imagine them cleaning off your biggest bubble, your
medium bubble, and your small bubble, and then
imagine these waters coming into your body.*

*As they work on cleansing you with these purify-
ing waters, imagine that your energy field begins to
expand far past even the building you're in. Gently
become aware of the parts of you that are so big, so
brilliant, so beautiful that they are beyond anything
that you can imagine.*

*Give the archangels permission to enter into all
aspects, all layers of your consciousness, all layers
of your mind, all layers of your heart and soul, so*

*that they can do their purifying work. This is what they do! This is what they are good at. This is their blessing to you today.*

*Accept their gift of purity into all layers of who you are, throughout all directions of space and time. Allow these purifying waters to rain and cascade down through all that you are.*

*Thank these archangels for their beautiful waters of purity and for this deep spiritual cleansing that you received today.*

When you are done with the meditation, stay sitting quietly, and read the following downloads. Only read aloud the ones that really speak to you — those that represent new thoughts and feelings that you would like the angels to gift to you.

### Day 9 Downloads

- I know that it's possible to live with a pure mind.
- I know what it feels like to live with a pure heart and mind.
- It is safe to reveal my pure nature in my life.
- It is safe to know who I am in my purest form.
- I know how to and what it feels like to live without toxic thinking.
- I know what it feels like to be cleansed.
- I know the Creator's definition of what it means to be cleansed.
- I am cleansed.

- I know how to and what it feels like to live with purity.
- I understand the Creator's definition of what purity is on all levels of my mind.
- I now accept the pure divinity of my own true nature.

Allow these new thoughts and feelings to enter all of your space, all levels of your mind, and every cell of your body. Thank dear Archangel Uriel and Archangel Zadkiel from the bottom of your heart for this loving transmission.

May you go out today and see beautiful expressions of the purest forms of light and love in your life. These are the true reflections of your own true nature. You may even want to take a bath or hop in a body of water today to help support the work that you did. And of course, keep your eyes peeled for any messages along the way.

Angel juju coming at you.

# DAY 10

———————— ❖ ————————

# Harmony
## *with Archangel Raguel*

It takes a lot of courage to move in the world with a commitment to both inner and outer harmony. Archangel Raguel is coming forward today to attune you to harmony to help make it a little easier for you.

Archangel Raguel has an amazing way of supporting your trickiest relationships. He helps with the ability to cultivate peace and let go of grudges with ease. His energy can also create inner harmony by balancing your chakras and the relationship between your heart, your mind, and your connection to Spirit.

To be honest, the relationship between your heart and your mind can often be the biggest source of conflict in your life, so what an amazing blessing this is to receive today!

Think of one person in your life who has hurt you, someone you probably need to do some healing work around — whether it's someone who is currently in your life or someone you've known in the past. Maybe it's someone who has abused you or someone who you felt took advantage of you or someone whom you've had some misunderstandings with and just can't seem to see eye to eye with.

It's amazing how quickly the angels can help you detox from the negative emotions about these problematic relationships. This one is going to be fun!

Please have a person in mind before you begin your invocation and healing today, and get ready for some loving support from Archangel Raguel. Bring on the harmony!

When you are ready to begin, find a quiet spot, center yourself, and recite this invocation aloud:

 *Day 10 Invocation*

> *Dear Creator of All That Is and Archangel Raguel,*
> *I ask that your loving energy come into my life, into my relationships, and into my energy body to help create a deep ripple of harmony in all my relationships, including my relationship with myself. I thank you for coming to me today, Archangel Raguel, to bring this amazing gift of light and of perfect harmony in all things.*

Next, either you can listen to the free guided meditation audio that I have provided to you for Day 10 or you can perform the following meditation on your own.

> *Audio meditation*
> *available at*
> *TheAngelExperimentAudios.com/Day10*

### Day 10 Meditation

*Imagine Archangel Raguel is standing right there with you after your invocation. Then envision the person you have had some troubles with also standing in the room with you. As they stand there with you, imagine a figure eight made of rainbow light coming down from above. Place yourself in one of the loops of that figure eight, and place the other person in the other loop. Imagine the figure eight swirling around you both, creating a circuit of energy between you, as Raguel stands there and supports this process.*

*Ask Archangel Raguel to please remove any energies of disharmony between you and this person, and also between you and anything else in your life that is creating discord. Use your breath to bring in the energy of harmony, and exhale anything else that stands in the way of you feeling harmonious in your life.*

*Know that this ribbon of rainbow energy, this figure eight, is going to stay with you and between you and this person. It will create a nice buffer and help remove any lower frequencies and emotional toxins between you both.*

*Next, imagine a rainbow light different from the figure eight coming from above and radiating into your body, into your chakras. This rainbow light will help harmonize all your chakras and get them in alignment for you. Allow this light to bring healing to your heart and mind so that they can work in harmony as well.*

When you are done with the meditation, stay sitting quietly, and read the following downloads. Only read aloud the ones that really speak to you — those that represent new thoughts and feelings that you would like the angels to gift to you.

### ✄ • *Day 10 Downloads*

- I know what it feels like to live without grudges.
- I radiate harmony in all my relationships.
- I know what it feels like to be in sync with the world around me.
- I know how to and what it feels like to be in perfect harmony with myself.
- I know how to and what it feels like to be in perfect harmony with others.

Sit and receive these wonderful beliefs and feelings. Thank Archangel Raguel for bringing you this beauty and healing.

Today, when you go out into the world, notice the harmony that is happening all around you. Slow down and let yourself perceive the beautiful orchestra of nature and life as it moves around you. Notice if any of your relationships seem suspiciously pleasant. Also notice how you feel about the person you visualized, and see if anything has shifted for you. You may already be beginning to experience that shift.

Write down your experiences and enjoy a heightened sense of harmony today.

Angel juju coming at you.

# DAY 11

❧

# **Playfulness**
## *with the Cherubim*

Today's practice is such a fun blessing to bring to you, and it's all thanks to the help of the loving cherubs. The Cherubim are an order of angels that are often depicted as childlike angels that look like sweet little babies or young children.

Often, they are seen as the angels that help us with romance, but today they wanted to come forward and bring you the attunement of playfulness. So who am I to argue? We're going to let them! When I channeled for this day, I heard so much giggling and laughter, I know that they just can't wait to bring you this gift!

One thing they showed me today was a vision of children, specifically the image of a child stumbling and falling while learning to walk. As you know, when babies fall when they are learning to walk, they just get up and try it again. It's not a big deal at all for them. They don't sit on the floor and throw a pity party, refusing to try again. They simply get back up and keep going at it until they get it right.

This childlike determination is a big part of the playfulness that the cherubs want to bring to you today. Children have a fierce determination to party, a fierce determination to master a new skill, and a fierce commitment to enjoy themselves, even when they are apparently failing at something over and over again. They stumble and fall and hurt themselves, and still manage to have fun, without punishing themselves for not being perfect.

How different would your life look if you playfully allowed yourself to be imperfect, to fumble around in apparent failure without mentally abusing yourself?

What would happen if you let yourself be a little more adventurous? Would you be more willing to start that new venture that you have been dreaming about? Move to a different city? Join the community theater? Let go of that relationship that has been weighing you down?

I'm so excited that the cherubs are here to help you lighten up about your life and bring in that playful energy that your sweet little soul just might be craving.

When you are ready to begin, find a quiet spot, center yourself, and recite this invocation aloud:

### ➤──· *Day 11 Invocation*

*Dear Creator and beautiful little cherubs,*
  *I ask you to come to me today to open my heart to the gift of playfulness, and to help lighten my load so that I can remember my divine and childlike nature and see the divinity and beauty of the world through*

*a child's playful eyes. I thank you for coming to me today to bring me this powerful attunement. Thank you, Creator, and thank you, sweet little cherubs.*

Next, either you can listen to the free guided meditation audio that I have provided to you for Day 11 or you can perform the following meditation on your own.

*Audio meditation*
*available at*
*TheAngelExperimentAudios.com/Day 11*

### Day 11 Meditation

*Feeling into your heart, find one sweet, giddy spot inside your body. It can be a tiny spot or a big spot, but take your time to find it. That giddiness is inside all of us, and it's the doorway into true playfulness. The angels want to help make that giddiness expand, multiply, and radiate into the world. You can bring giddiness and playfulness into anything.*

*Find that part of your body, and imagine that there's a swirl of children around you, flying around you, laughing and giggling. Allow the energy of this laughter and giggling to activate that playful child in every cell of your body, so that every cell in your body is laughing and giggling.*

When you are done with the meditation, stay sitting quietly, and read the following downloads. Only read aloud the ones that really speak to you — those that represent new thoughts and feelings that you would like the angels to gift to you.

## Day 11 Downloads

- I remember who I am.
- I remember how to be a child.
- I know what it feels like to be a child and to be childlike.
- I know how to and what it feels like to play in my life.
- I know how to and what it feels like to play at my work.
- I know how to and what it feels like to play in all my relationships.
- I am playful.
- I know how to and what it feels like to let myself laugh out loud anytime.
- My life is a magical playground.

Thank these sweet, joyful cherubs; thank them for bringing their playfulness to you. Then bring your awareness more fully back into the room.

You have been blessed today with the attitude of play. Know that your life is truly a magical playground. So get out there, get dirty, and make sure to laugh about it! Also, write down any inspired ideas or any playful circumstances that come up for you today.

Angel juju coming at you.

# DAY 12

— ❧ —

# Gratitude

## *with Archangel Sandalphon*

Today's invocation is about the angels thanking you for all your courage, for all the help you've given others, and for being an example of the endurance, power, and strength that it takes to persevere in life even under the worst kinds of strife.

Today, the angels are honoring you, understanding how difficult it is to be human and to be surrounded by all manner of trials and tribulations They want you to know that you are a love warrior, and they see that you are fighting for love. This is the good fight.

They thank you for the extra love and sparkle that you bring to your loved ones, to your friends, and to your communities — and, boy, does the world need it! It takes special muscle to still give light and love to others even when the world around you can sometimes be sucky, harsh, and straight-up clueless.

The angels want you to know that you and your heart are a true gift on this planet, and the angels and I want to help you open your heart even more, so that you can receive this gift of gratitude that the angels are giving you today.

When you are ready to begin, find a quiet spot, center yourself, and recite this invocation aloud:

### ⟩—• Day 12 Invocation

*Dear Creator, Archangel Sandalphon, and the rest of the archangels,*

*Help me to open my heart to fully receive your gratitude today so that I can finally understand, see, and feel my own value in the world, and so that the gifts that I give and receive may multiply in my life and in the lives of all of those around me. Thank you, Archangel Sandalphon and other archangels, for bringing me this gift today.*

Next, either you can listen to the free guided meditation audio that I have provided to you for Day 12 or you can perform the following meditation on your own.

*Audio meditation available at TheAngelExperimentAudios.com/Day12*

### ⟩—• Day 12 Meditation

*Bring your attention into your heart and imagine a cup, an empty cup. See that beautiful cup sitting inside your heart. Next, invite Archangel Sandalphon to come and fill your cup with gratitude. In order to receive gratitude, you must first be receptive, so imagine that this cup in your heart is a symbol of pure receptivity, as if it's saying, "I am here to receive." You have been doing so much good in your life, and this is your moment to receive gratitude from the angels.*

*Remembering to breathe, watch as the energy of gratitude comes to your space and starts filling your cup. Allow Archangel Sandalphon and the other archangels to come and give their thanks for the hard work that you've been doing. Again, they understand how hard life can be. They are giving you great respect and honoring you for the sacrifices you've made to be here. Welcome in this gratitude.*

*Next, imagine that every cell in your body is a teeny-tiny cup, so that each can receive this gratitude from the archangels today.*

*The angels are so thankful for your faith and for your hope, because without you they would not be able to do their work of light and love.*

*They're bringing you this message today so that when you step out into the world, you know what your mission is.*

*Your mission is to be and spread the light. To do that, you must take the time to receive the light, so this is your chance.*

*Exhale anything that gets in the way of you truly feeling this gratitude.*

When you are done with the meditation, stay sitting quietly, and read the following downloads. Only read aloud the ones that really speak to you — those that

represent new thoughts and feelings that you would like the angels to gift to you.

### ✂ ⋅ *Day 12 Downloads*

- I know how to see myself and my life as a gift.
- I know what it feels like to be cherished.
- It is safe to feel valued, and it is safe to feel cherished.
- I know how to value, cherish, and respect myself.
- I know how to receive compliments and gratitude from others with ease and grace.
- I know how to feel truly deserving of gratitude.

Next, take some breaths as you imagine those new thoughts and feelings coming down and resting in all levels of your mind, your heart, your body, and your spirit. Allow this offering of gratitude to permeate the space around you, into your aura.

Today, know that you are cherished and deeply valued by your guardians and by the angels. As you walk out into your day, do so with an extra pep in your step, knowing that you belong here and that the world needs you. Your angelic helpers are so grateful for you! Today, realize just how much of a gift you have been, and feel free to write down anything that comes to you.

Angel juju coming at you.

# DAY 13

❧

# Divine Purpose

## *with Archangel Michael*

I am so excited about this very special day! Yesterday, you received so much gratitude from the angels, and today, you're going to discover why. It's because you came here for a sacred purpose.

Believe it or not, we all come here for a reason. You may already know your purpose, or this might be the first time you are considering this. In either case, today's attunement will open you up to the next level of your purpose, as you continue to unfold and expand like a beautiful flower blossoming into the world. There is always room for growth, and there are always new layers to discover.

This is what the angels were talking to you about yesterday. They honor the sacrifice you have made to take on this purpose, this mission in life, and have its effects ripple out to the lives around you.

Archangel Michael governs life purpose, so he wanted to come today to help open you up even more to your divine purpose and the blueprint of your mission here. He wants you to know that so many of you who are reading this book are special souls that came here for a specific mission to help usher the light and love into the world in your own unique and specific way.

Today's experience will help you align with your deeper soul purpose, to create even more space in your world so you can fulfill the entirety of your mission here.

When you are ready to begin, find a quiet spot, center yourself, and recite this invocation aloud:

### • Day 13 Invocation

*Dear Creator and Archangel Michael,*

*I thank you for coming to me today to help me realize that I am here for a purpose. I ask that you resolve and clear any blocks that prevent me from fully understanding and knowing my purpose, and I also ask that you give me the courage to fulfill my divine soul mission. I thank you, Creator and Archangel Michael, for this amazing gift today.*

Next, either you can listen to the free guided meditation audio that I have provided to you for Day 13 or you can perform the following meditation on your own.

*Audio meditation available at TheAngelExperimentAudios.com/Day13*

## ·*Day 13 Meditation*

*Imagine Archangel Michael is standing with you. Allow him to begin to open you up and attune your body to nothing outside yourself, but only to your unique vibration, your true essence.*

*Imagine a beautiful color coming into your space that represents your unique vibration, and remember this color. Allow yourself to experience this color, your beautiful radiance, by breathing it into your body, your organs, and your bones. Next, imagine Archangel Michael standing by to help you attune to your unique purpose and power, to the true blueprint of your origin, of your soul, and to help you decode and remember who you are and what you came here to do.*

*Envision Archangel Michael melting away any thick crust, residue, or debris covering that blueprint, or any fear you may have about knowing the truth about you. Imagine that he is opening you up to your own true essence, which is radiant and powerful like a star shining in the night sky.*

When you are done with the meditation, stay sitting quietly, and read the following downloads. Only read aloud the ones that really speak to you — those that represent new thoughts and feelings that you would like the angels to gift to you.

## ·*Day 13 Downloads*

- I know what it feels like to live with divine purpose.

- I have a unique purpose.
- I am here for a purpose.
- I matter, and my purpose matters.
- It's safe to know my true purpose.
- I know my true purpose.
- It is safe to fulfill my true purpose, and I know how to do so with courage, with ease, and with flow.

Remember to breathe and imagine you are getting peppered with goodness from the heavens. Thank Archangel Michael for helping you align with your true essence and for activating your divine purpose.

As you go out into your day today, allow yourself to receive signs and clues about your mission here. If you're not consciously aware of what your mission is, be curious and ask yourself questions like "If I have a mission here, what is it?" Sometimes it's not what you think.

Be sure to write down any insights, information, or synchronicities that come to you today, as those could be breadcrumbs leading you to a deeper under-standing of who you are and what exactly you came here to do.

Angel juju coming at you.

# DAY 14

--------- ⚜ ---------

# Protection
## *with Archangel Michael*

Today is the second day that Archangel Michael is coming in to support your spiritual path and your mission. Today's invocation is important for everyone, and especially those who had challenging or abusive parents and grew up never feeling fully safe.

Many of us carry around unconscious imprints and memories of feeling unsafe as children, and this anxiety can block us from being at peace in our lives and from fully being able to fulfill our missions.

Archangel Michael wants to correct all that today. He wants to send you the energy and the shield of loving and divine protection, not just to you today as an adult, but to you at every age, all the way back to when you were still in your mama's tummy.

Archangel Michael is going to be very thorough today so that all parts of you know that it is safe to come out to play in the world. He wants to show you that you have powerful protection around you, now and always, from this day forward.

When you are ready to begin, find a quiet spot, center yourself, and recite this invocation aloud:

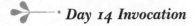 *Day 14 Invocation*

*Dear Creator of All That Is and Archangel Michael,*
*    Please come to me today to bring me the gift of divine protection. I thank you so much for helping me feel and know in every cell of my body that you are with me and that I am eternally safe. Thank you, Creator and Archangel Michael, for this special gift.*

Next, either you can listen to the free guided meditation audio that I have provided to you for Day 14 or you can perform the following meditation on your own.

*Audio meditation*
*available at*
*TheAngelExperimentAudios.com/Day14*

*Day 14 Meditation*

*Close your eyes, and allow your body to sense the energy of protection surrounding you. Allow yourself to see or feel this powerful presence with you. It might come as an image, as a powerful sensation, as a very gentle or light sensation, or in some other form, unique to you. Be very still and notice as Archangel Michael brings his powerful shield of protection to you.*

*Imagine that he sends that energy of protection backward in time to all those moments when you did not feel safe, at every age of your life, all the way back to when you were in your mother's belly.*

*Thank Archangel Michael for sending you his light and love to protect you during every moment when you got the message that you were not safe, from your conception all the way until today. All those messages were lies, and, in fact, according to Archangel Michael, you are and always have been eternally safe. Archangel Michael is helping you understand and feel this truth at the deepest level of your mind. Witness all this protection entering every aspect of yourself and your life.*

When you are done with the meditation, stay sitting quietly, and read the following downloads. Only read aloud the ones that really speak to you — those that represent new thoughts and feelings that you would like the angels to gift to you. After you read each of your downloads aloud, breathe in to deeply receive and embody the thought and feeling it conveys.

### Day 14 Downloads

- I'm protected by light and love now.
- I know what it feels like to always be protected, in this moment and in every moment.
- I see that I have always been protected.
- I can see how well I am protected now.

- I know how to move in the world feeling eternally protected.
- I am protected.
- I am safe.
- My family is eternally safe.

Thank Archangel Michael, all his helpers, and the Creator for this wonderful blessing of divine protection.

May you walk out into the world today feeling stronger, standing tall and knowing that you've got a major invisible posse at your back that is helping you along and protecting you at every turn. Notice what shifted for you today and write anything and everything down.

Angel juju coming at you.

# DAY 15

———— ✤ ————

# Courage

*with Archangel Ariel
and Archangel Michael*

Today's dynamic duo, Archangels Ariel and Michael are showing up just in time as you begin to open up more to your true self and your true mission. It's one thing to live your life, but it is a whole different thing to live your life to the fullest.

In order to live life to the fullest, you'll need extra doses of courage because breaking out of the old way of doing things just isn't easy, and to be frank, sometimes it can be straight-up scary.

I am happy that Archangels Michael and Ariel are here to help bring you courage today, because they are angelic badasses, and you will need their strength to help you walk like a boss toward the life of your dreams.

When you are ready to begin, find a quiet spot, center yourself, and recite this invocation aloud:

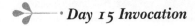 **Day 15 Invocation**

> *Dear Creator, Archangel Ariel, and Archangel Michael,*
> *Thank you for coming to me today to help trans-*
> *form my fears into fierceness. Give me the courage to*
> *let nothing stop me from making the changes I know*
> *I need to make in my life, and the courage to let go of*
> *anything in my life that I've outgrown. Thank you,*
> *Ariel and Michael, for coming to me today.*

Next, either you can listen to the free guided meditation audio that I have provided to you for Day 15 or you
can perform the following meditation on your own.

> *Audio meditation*
> *available at*
> *TheAngelExperimentAudios.com/Day15*

**Day 15 Meditation**

> *Place your attention on your body and how it is feel-*
> *ing. Imagine Archangels Ariel and Michael stand-*
> *ing right there with you. See, feel, or sense them, and*
> *notice in your body any shift or change that happens*
> *as you make contact with these powerful angels.*
> *You might feel tingles. You might start heating*
> *up. Or maybe you simply feel energy around you.*
> *Whatever it is, focus on any physical feeling that*
> *happens for you.*
> *Envision that these two archangels have brought*
> *you two very important items — one is a sword and*

*one is a shield. Imagine them handing you the sword, a sword so beautiful that you've never seen anything like it. Then imagine that you take that sword and hold it in your hand.*

*Next, imagine you are receiving a shield with a very special insignia on it. It could be an animal. It could just be a shape. It could be anything. Let yourself perceive what the insignia is, and trust the first vision that comes to you. That insignia is going to be your special symbol for courage and strength.*

*As you hold this shield and sword in your hands, let the angels move out any fear that's stuck in your body, any fear that's preventing you from moving forward in your life, trying to trick you into believing that you don't have the courage.*

*Breathe deeply as the angels move this old, fearful energy out of you. Give it to them freely and say, "Take this from me now in exchange for courage and strength."*

*The sword will help you cut away all your limited thinking, the cobwebs of anything that's old, anything that you've outgrown.*

*The shield will protect you from negativity from the outside world, from the perceptions of others, from the fear and worry of others, so that you can be eternally safe and impervious to such negativity.*

*Witness as Archangels Ariel and Michael continue to move old energy out of you, all the way down to your bones.*

When you are done with the meditation, stay sitting quietly, and read the following downloads. Only read aloud the ones that really speak to you — those that

represent new thoughts and feelings that you would like the angels to gift to you.

### *Day 15 Downloads*

- I know what it feels like to be strong in every cell of my body.
- I know how it feels for my bones to be strong, for my back to be strong.
- I know what it feels like to have the divine at my back, helping me move forward.
- I know how to and what it feels like to truly be determined on my path.
- I know how to and what it feels like to be fierce in my life.
- I know how to turn my fear into fierceness.
- I know how to and when to move forward in my life, even when I am afraid.
- I am ready to move forward fearlessly now.

Breathe in these new thoughts and feelings, and know that you are now armed and ready to be that fierce warrior of love. Thank Archangel Michael and Archangel Ariel for this amazing work.

Now you are armed with extraordinary tools and courage to help you along your path. Today, see how courage shows up in your world. You'll also want to take time to draw the insignia that you received in today's transmission so that you'll have a record of it and can use it however you want when you need an extra dose of courage.

Angel juju coming at you.

# DAY 16

———— ❖ ————

# Passion

*with Archangel Haniel*

Boy, oh boy! Today's attunement is such a hot one. It will help you awaken your true passions and bring more juiciness into your life. So delish! Who doesn't need more passion in their life, right?

So many people I talk to unfortunately don't even know what their passions are. They have been so focused on their responsibilities and the roles that they play as adults that often their passions have been buried, sacrificed in exchange for practicality. Yuck!

I love this gift from the angels, because really all that the angels want for you is happiness, but it's challenging to be happy if you've forgotten what *makes* you happy. Do you know what you are passionate about? What are your passions? If there is radio silence in that sweet little noggin of yours, then the angels are urging you to remember. It's time to reawaken your passion, and today we are doing it with Archangel Haniel.

When you are ready to begin, find a quiet spot, center yourself, and recite this invocation aloud:

### Day 16 Invocation

*Dear Creator of All That Is and Archangel Haniel,*
    *I thank you for filling every area of my life with passion. Please help me awaken the passion in my love relationships, in my friendships, in my career, and in my body so I can experience true fulfillment and true ecstasy in all my endeavors. I thank you, Archangel Haniel.*

Next, either you can listen to the free guided meditation audio that I have provided to you for Day 16 or you can perform the following meditation on your own.

*Audio meditation available at TheAngelExperimentAudios.com/Day16*

### Day 16 Meditation

*To start, visualize Archangel Haniel standing with you as she invites you on a journey with her below the surface of the earth. Picture yourself going down past the soil, past the rocks, past the water, into the vast sea of hot magma that flows beneath the earth's crust. Imagine being immersed in this hot, fiery liquid. Though it is hot, the molten rock doesn't burn you but instead energizes you and activates your inner passion. Envision Archangel Haniel beside you, opening up space for you to be a true channel of divine passion.*

*As you breathe, inhale the fiery liquid up from the ground, through the bottom of your feet, and let it flow through your entire body. Now bring your awareness to your tailbone and pelvic region, until it merges with the "fire in your belly," your inherent passion and drive.*

*Welcome this energy of passion back into your life and feel it penetrate every cell of your body until you are completely filled up. Allow the magma to overflow from the top of your skull through your crown chakra and cascade over your physical body like warm, delicious honey.*

When you are done with the meditation, stay sitting quietly, and read the following downloads. Only read aloud the ones that really speak to you — those that represent new thoughts and feelings that you would like the angels to gift to you.

### Day 16 Downloads

- I know how to be passionate.
- I know what it feels like to be passionate.
- I am filled with passion.
- It's safe for me to be passionate and to show my passion.
- I feel passion in every cell of my body.

- It's safe to know all my true passions.
- I'm worthy of having passion in my life.
- I know how to and what it feels like to live my passion.

Allow yourself to receive and breathe in these downloads. Allow these new thoughts and feelings to swirl in every cell of your body, just like the magma swirled in every cell of your body during the meditation. And thank the earth and Archangel Haniel for hooking you up with this goodness.

Today, become aware of passion and how it expresses itself in your life.

Give yourself permission to have a passion-filled day, and make sure to keep a record of any new or old passions that start bubbling up for you.

Angel juju coming at you.

# DAY 17

—— ✤ ——

# **Wealth**

*with Archangel Ariel*

Today's special healing from the angels is one that none of us would kick out of bed. Archangel Ariel is here to help you with a little thing called wealth. Want to improve your wealth quotient? Here is the channeled message from Archangel Ariel to give you her spin on wealth and how she's going to help you with it today:

> *Dear Children of Light,*
> *Open your arms to profound magic, dear beautiful ones. You stand as creators in this world, and it is time to create. Your magical wealth lies not in your wallet or in your bank account or in your job, but in your divine nature. You are your own source of abundance. Look nowhere outside yourself. Allow the fountain of gold to spring from within you as your true source of wealth. Drink from the cup within you as I, your higher self, and your Creator help you to open up to this divine spring of wealth and abundance that is within you.*

Thank you, Ariel, for that message.

When you are ready to begin, find a quiet spot, center yourself, and recite this invocation aloud:

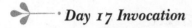 *Day 17 Invocation*

*Dear Creator and Archangel Ariel,*

*I ask that you come to me today and open up the divine spring of wealth that is within me. Help me dissolve any blocks that stop me from opening to the abundant flow of divine wealth within me and in my daily life. Help me be a magnet for wealth in all its beautiful forms. Thank you, Ariel.*

Next, either you can listen to the free guided meditation audio that I have provided to you for Day 17 or you can perform the following meditation on your own.

*Audio meditation available at TheAngelExperimentAudios.com/Day17*

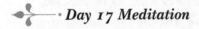 *Day 17 Meditation*

*Connect with your heart by dropping your awareness into it.*

*Investigate your heart and the space that it resides in. Notice if you find any tightness or heaviness there. Now see sparkling golden liquid light radiating within your heart. Archangel Ariel and your guides are here to help you open up to the divine wealth and abundance that are within you and that come from the heart.*

*Allow this golden liquid to open up and flow like a beautiful fountain. See it start flowing like a golden spring within you. Watch as that spring becomes more powerful until its flow feels just right for you. Take your time, and don't force it. The energy will flow eventually, so sit with it until it does.*

*Allow that spring to flow abundantly within you until your whole body is full of this golden spring.*

*Next, allow this beautiful golden light to flow out in every direction in your life. Allow this spring to flow into your bank accounts.*

*Allow this spring to flow into your wallet. Imagine all your credit cards there. Allow that beautiful, divine spring of wealth to touch every single one of your credit cards.*

*Allow it to touch your paychecks, to touch your job and your environment around the job. And now, allow this flow to touch your relationships so that you can feel divine wealth in your relationships.*

*Breathe deeply and invite the angels to remove any blocks that you would like to dissolve, especially those blocks that have been keeping you from knowing your true wealth. Imagine that you're sitting in a golden throne surrounded by jewels, surrounded by golden coins, and invite this wealth into all layers of your mind, heart, body, and spirit.*

When you are done with the meditation, stay sitting quietly, and read the following downloads. Only read aloud the ones that really speak to you — those that represent new thoughts and feelings that you would like the angels to gift to you.

### Day 17 Downloads

- I know how to and what it feels like to be wealthy in all levels of my mind and in every cell of my body.
- I am an abundant source of wealth and richness.
- I am a wealth magnet.
- My life flows with abundance.
- In every aspect of my life, I am a magnet for wealth.
- I'm freaky rich.

That's right, freaky rich. Yes! As these downloads come to you, know that you are surrounded by all the benevolent beings of wealth across the world, welcoming you to your throne of divine wealth. Watch as they place a regal gown of divine wealth around you. When you are finished, thank Archangel Ariel and all the other beings of wealth for today's lesson in opening up to the true source of abundance.

Today, as you walk in the world, wear your regal gown of divine wealth and know that all your needs are met and then some. Become aware of how your cup is already full in your life. This will help the energy of wealth move more freely.

Spend some time journaling about your feelings about wealth, and ask your angels to continue to remove any beliefs that limit your capacity to hold more wealth in your life.

Angel juju coming at you.

# DAY 18

— ❧ —

# Divine Health

## *with Archangel Raphael*
## *and Archangel Uriel*

Having mental or physical health struggles? Help is on the way. According to Spirit, our bodies are capable of way more than what our minds and belief systems can currently comprehend. For Day 18 the angels are dropping down some health wisdom for you — they will be working to activate perfect and divine health within your DNA. Say what? Yes, your DNA. Today, keep an open mind and receive the delightful gift that the angels have for you. Your body will thank you.

Here's a channeled message from Archangel Uriel and Archangel Raphael for today:

*Dear ones,*

*Today, we see your perfection. We see you in perfect health. Your divine health is the truth. This body that you're in is actually designed for perfect health. It is designed for immortality. Today, allow us to awaken these codes of perfect and divine health so you can understand your body and mind's miraculous ability to heal swiftly and with ease. Right now, surrender your aches, surrender your anguish, surrender any physical pain, and allow the truth of divine health to emerge in every cell of your body, in all layers of your mind.*

Thank you, archangels.

When you are ready to begin, find a quiet spot, center yourself, and recite this invocation aloud:

### ◆—— • *Day 18 Invocation*

*Dear Creator of All That Is, Archangel Raphael, and Archangel Uriel,*

*Thank you for coming to me today to help me experience divine balance and health in all its forms, in every cell of my body and in every level of my mind. I ask that you clear me of any influences that are creating disease in my body or in my mind in exchange for perfect and divine health. I thank you, Archangel Raphael and Archangel Uriel.*

Next, either you can listen to the free guided meditation audio that I have provided to you for Day 18 or you can perform the following meditation on your own.

*Audio meditation available at TheAngelExperimentAudios.com/Day18*

## · *Day 18 Meditation*

*Bring your awareness to your body and how it is feeling right now. Imagine that these beautiful celestial doctors, Archangels Raphael and Uriel, come to you and touch certain parts of your body that need the most support.*

*Sometimes you can feel them there, and sometimes you can simply close your eyes and imagine where they are touching you. Wherever it is, trust that the angels are there with you and that they are removing any physical and mental disease from you.*

*Breathe deeply while you surrender any physical pain and any aches to these celestial doctors, and ask that they remove the source of these aches now. You don't even have to know what the source of the discomfort is; all you have to do is ask.*

*Allow the miracle of deep and profound healing to enter your body and your mind. You can say out loud, "Yes. Take this from me. I ask for perfect and divine health now."*

When you are done with the meditation, stay sitting quietly, and read the following downloads. Only read aloud the ones that really speak to you — those that represent new thoughts and feelings that you would like the angels to gift to you.

## ✂ • *Day 18 Downloads*

- I give permission to activate my DNA codes for perfect and divine health.
- I know what it feels like to have a happy and healthy body.
- I know what it feels like to have a happy and healthy mind.
- I'm worthy of having a happy and healthy body.
- I'm worthy of having a happy and healthy mind.
- It's my divine birthright to be whole and healthy now.
- I know how to live without pain, and it is possible for me.
- My body feels alive, limber, strong, and free.
- I know what it means to be disease-free.
- I know what it feels like to be disease-free.
- My mind feels balanced and clear.
- I know the Creator's definition of perfect and divine health.
- I know how to have an instant healing.

As these new feelings and beliefs come to you, breathe deeply while you accept them into every cell of your body. Know that as you sit, the codes of perfection, the codes of perfect and divine health, are awakening in your DNA in every cell of your body. Thank Archangels Uriel and Raphael for coming to help you experience your own divine perfection.

Return to today's practice as often as you need to. Allow this work to continue penetrating every level and layer of your mind. Keep your awareness focused on your health today. Notice if any positive mental or physical changes happen for you today. Are you feeling as achy? As depressed? As anxious? Become aware of any positive movement that happens for you, and make sure to write it down.

Angel juju coming at you.

# DAY 19

—— ✢ ——

# Divine Love
## *with the Seraphim*

The Seraphim are an angelic order, and the root of their name, *śārāf* in Hebrew, means "love." The Seraphim are the perfect ones to show you what divine love truly means. As I closed my eyes to channel for this day, the angels showed me two gorgeous lovers surrounded by brilliant white light and gazing into each other's eyes while dancing. The love between them was palpable and passionate.

What the Seraphim want you to understand is that divine love is like a dance between two passionate lovers, between you and the other, between you and nature, between you and your loved ones, between you and the divine, and between you and life itself.

Here's a channeled message from the Seraphim for today:

*Beautiful child,*
*Open your arms to your life and embrace it as*
*if it were your truest and most passionate lover. As*

*you do this, you will become infused with the truth of divine love in all things. The divine is alive in your life right now, so let it love you deeply. Open your arms to profound, powerful, and divine love from us and from your Creator. Today and every day, you are worthy of this love, beautiful child, sweet innocent Child of Light.*

Well, thank you, Seraphim.

When you are ready to begin, find a quiet spot, center yourself, and recite this invocation aloud:

### ➤ Day 19 Invocation

*Dear holy order of the Seraphim, you who are closest to our Creator, you who are divine love manifested,*

*I thank you for breathing the fire of divine love into every aspect of my life, my mind, and my heart. I ask for your help today in opening up all of me to even deeper love so that I may dance with life and with the divine. I thank you today for this powerful gift.*

Next, either you can listen to the free guided meditation audio that I have provided to you for Day 19 or you can perform the following meditation on your own.

*Audio meditation available at TheAngelExperimentAudios.com/Day19*

## Day 19 Meditation

*Imagine that giant, beautiful, golden beings are in the room with you, surrounding you. Their radiance is so bright that it fills the room.*

*Breathe in the divine love that they are bringing you today.*

*Literally open your arms to receive this love. You can extend your arms, with your palms facing up, to receive the love that's in the room.*

*Allow the warmth to open up new routes and new chambers in your heart. Allow this powerful golden radiance to permeate any aches and pains in your body, to melt away your worries and concerns, and to shine so brightly that the darkness has no chance to live inside you. Let this light surround every part of you that feels like it needs that love.*

When you are done with the meditation, stay sitting quietly, and read the following downloads. Only read aloud the ones that really speak to you — those that represent new thoughts and feelings that you would like the angels to gift to you.

## Day 19 Downloads

- I know the Creator's definition of divine love.
- I am a powerful conduit for divine love.
- I know how to live from the fountain of love.
- I know what it feels like to do the dance of love in my life.
- I am worthy of profound love.

- I am deeply loved by life.
- I love my life deeply.
- I know how to allow myself to be deeply loved
  by my life.
- I open myself now to higher forms of love than
  I have ever known.

As these new thoughts and feelings come into the deepest layers of your heart and mind, know that you are loved and capable of profound love. Know that you're good at giving love and good at receiving love. Thank the Seraphim for this beautiful gift.

When you walk out into the world today, see the reflection and the bounty of love in every area of your life. Let this love dance with you, and notice just how much life loves you back. Document any love experiences that happen for you today.

Angel juju coming at you.

# DAY 20

———— ⚜ ————

# **Brilliance**

## *with the Seraphim*

The Seraphim are showing up now, near the end of this wonderful angel experiment, as they are truly the ones closest to the Creator and they radiate pure light. The Seraphim are also called "the burning ones" or "the shining ones," so they are the perfect beings to deliver us a gift of brilliance. They want you to shine your radiance, your brilliance, into the world.

They showed me how from Day 1 until now, it has been like a deep cleansing of 20 different facets of a beautiful diamond. They showed me that this sparkling, beautiful, and perfect diamond is your soul.

What this work is doing for you is actually uncovering the light of your spirit and the light of Source within you, so that it can shine more freely through you and out into the world. What a beautiful thing.

Here is a short channeled message for you today from the Seraphim:

*Shine your light. Shine your light, beautiful child of the stars, for all to see — unbridled, breathtaking, and brilliant. Shine your light, shine your life, and shine your love.*

Simple but awesome. Thank you, Seraphim!

When you are ready to begin, find a quiet spot, center yourself, and recite this invocation aloud:

### ❧— • *Day 20 Invocation*

*Dear beautiful ones, shining ones, burning ones, great Seraphim, and Creator,*

*I call upon you today to shower me with divine brilliance, to make me an even purer vessel to hold the light of Source. I ask you to melt away anything that stands in the way of my knowing my true brilliance and anything that prevents me from shining my brilliance into the world. I thank you for coming to me today, great Seraphim.*

Next, either you can listen to the free guided meditation audio that I have provided to you for Day 20 or you can perform the following meditation on your own.

*Audio meditation
available at
TheAngelExperimentAudios.com/Day20*

## Day 20 Meditation

*Imagine those same Seraphim from yesterday coming to you today to bless you, to open up a direct pathway between you and your Creator. Envision a beam of brilliant white light coming from deep in space. This light comes down from the heavens as sparkly, luminescent light. Allow this light, this unconditional love, to beam into the top of your head.*

*Imagine this light coming down through the top of your head into your body and shining in all directions through you like a kaleidoscope of light.*

*Allow this light to melt away any obstructions. Allow it to purify you, to cleanse anything that needs to be cleansed today so that you can be a more powerful conduit of Source, of unconditional love, and of brilliance in the world.*

When you are done with the meditation, stay sitting quietly, and read the following downloads. Only read aloud the ones that really speak to you — those that represent new thoughts and feelings that you would like the angels to gift to you.

## Day 20 Downloads

- I know the Creator's definition of brilliance.
- I am radiant.
- I know what it feels like to be radiant.
- I know how to attract my deepest desires through my radiance.

- I am a star.
- I know how to be my own star.
- I remember who I am.
- I am a powerful conduit for the brilliance of the Creator.

As these new thoughts and feelings wash through you and enter your mind and every cell of your body, focus on your breath. Know that there is no work to be done, that shining your light requires no work. It simply is. Sit in the place of just *being* your radiance without having to do, do, do. Thank the Seraphim for this great blessing today.

Today, when you go out into the world, let go of working so hard to be something for others or to make something happen. Let your only work be to shine your natural radiance in the world. That is truly enough, so let it flow.

May this brilliance be reflected in all you do today, and pay special attention to how others and the world around you respond to you. Keep writing down any angel experiences along the way.

One more angel attunement to go!

Angel juju coming at you.

# DAY 21

———— ❧ ————

# Joy
## *with Archangel Haniel*

Can you believe it's already Day 21? Time flies when you are partying with the angels.

Today's attunement is coming from Archangel Haniel, and the Principalities and the Virtues — two very powerful orders of angels that want to team up with Archangel Haniel on your behalf.

Today's healing is the perfect one to leave you with as we wind down these angel-inspired days.

Archangel Haniel is here to encourage you to stop looking for joy in people or circumstances outside yourself, mostly because these sources of joy can never truly stay reliable or consistent. The outside circumstances in our lives change all too much with the natural ebbs and flows of nature.

Her message to you today is to know that the work you've done over these 21 days is meant to support you in everlasting joy and to give you divine strength. It is only this connection with yourself and with the divine that will allow you to know a true joy that is both sustaining and eternal.

When you are ready to begin, find a quiet spot, center yourself, and recite this invocation aloud:

### Day 21 Invocation

*Dear Creator, Archangel Haniel, and all the Principalities and Virtues,*

*I ask you to help awaken the true source of joy within me. And I ask that this joy be sustained throughout my life, forever and always. I thank you for coming and sharing the vibration of everlasting joy with me.*

Next, either you can listen to the free guided meditation audio that I have provided to you for Day 21 or you can perform the following meditation on your own.

*Audio meditation available at TheAngelExperimentAudios.com/Day21*

### Day 21 Meditation

*Invite the Principalities, the Virtues, and Archangel Haniel to come to you. Visualize, hear, or feel them applauding, singing, and laughing with abundant joy. Imagine that their laughter is creating symphonies, beautiful music, joyful music. Imagine that this music, this symphony, is permeating the space you're in and the world around you.*

*Witness as this music and this joyous laughter radiate all around the world — to every country, through all the oceans, all the trees, to all the animals and all the humans — because today is a day of celebration, for you have completed this very special journey. I want you to know how celebrated you are!*

*Bring your awareness to your body, and allow your body to absorb vibrations of joy's movement. See it moving through your eyes, so that every vision can be filled with joy; through your ears, so that your ears can perceive levels of joy through sound; through your skin, so that your skin can be sensitive to the frequency and vibrations of joy; and through your sense of smell, so that you can become enlivened with the joyful aromas of the world around you and in your life.*

*Allow this joy to touch every cell of your body and all the spaces in between your cells. Let the choir of joy, the symphony of joy, reach into every piece of you and every layer of your soul, of your mind, of your heart. Allow this beautiful symphony of joy to reverberate through your body, through your heart, through your mind.*

When you are done with the meditation, stay sitting quietly, and read the following downloads. Only read aloud the ones that really speak to you — those that

represent new thoughts and feelings that you would like the angels to gift to you.

## ✂— • *Day 21 Downloads*

- I know what it feels like to experience the symphony of joy in my body.
- I know what it feels like to experience the symphony of joy in my mind and in my heart.
- I know how to feel joy.
- I know how to recognize that I'm surrounded by joy.
- I can feel the joy in others.
- I can feel the joy in nature.
- I can feel the joy of the divine.
- I know what it feels like to hear and feel the angels sing.
- I know what it feels like to bring the gift of joy into the world around me, into my family, and into my communities.
- I understand that the source of joy lives within me.
- I know how to step into the frequency of joy easily.
- I am joy in every cell of my body.
- I know how to live my life in joy.
- I know how to spread joy to everyone around me.
- I'm truly worthy of joy.
- I know how to receive true joy now.

Breathe in these feelings and thoughts now. Thank Archangel Haniel, the Principalities, and the Virtues for bringing this blessing of joy to you and to the world around you.

Today, as you go out into the world, allow this joy to move through you and be reflected back into every area of your life. Notice the joy in the animals, humans, and other life around you, and know that all the good work you have done during this angel experiment will continue to multiply in your life.

Angel juju coming at you!

But wait! Before we end, I have one more day for you: bonus Day 22. It's the perfect way to tie the bow around the sacred work that you have accomplished over the past 21 days, so make sure to complete it.

# BONUS: DAY 22

——————— ⚜ ———————

# Reflections and Gratitude

You did it! Congrats on completing this 21-day journey!

Now that you have successfully conducted the official 21-day angel experiment, it's time to take a closer look at the findings you have gathered with the archangels.

You know all those notes and journal entries I had you write down? I want you to spend some time now to analyze the data that you have collected thus far. I want you to look through your notes, beginning with Day 1, and read everything you have written. Much of it you may have forgotten about already.

Make sure to review *all* your notes carefully. Take your time with this so that you don't miss anything.

In reviewing all your findings, what did you discover and observe over these 21 days with your angels? Answer these questions:

• Did any particular themes come up for you? Any repeating messages or experiences?

- Did any synchronicities happen in your life?
- Were you inspired to do new things, make new connections, or make some changes in direction in your life?
- Did you notice feeling more peaceful, more connected, more supported, more energetic, more youthful, or happier?
- Did any mind-blowing unexplainable things happen for you?
- Did you seem to have more good luck?
- Have any mental or physical health conditions improved?
- Did any of your relationships improve?
- How do you feel about your life right now versus how you felt about it 21 days ago?

A lot can happen in 21 days, especially when the angels get involved, so take the time to absorb all the goodness that has transpired for you so that I can give you one last step to fully complete this angel experiment.

Now that you have reviewed all your notes and analyzed all the divine data that you have accrued over the days, it's time for me to ask you one final question:

Based on your findings…are angels real?

If your answer is yes, then a cosmic fist bump to you. Bam! Your angel magic is officially flowing. Thank your angels wholeheartedly, and ask them to keep showing you just how real they are.

If your answer is no, or you still aren't sure, then no worries. We still have time, and like any good scientist, you may need to keep on experimenting.

In either case, in the last part of this book, I will show you ways that you can continue the good work you have started with your angels so that you can keep strengthening your bond with them and keep raising your life to the highest possible vibration.

# CONCLUSION

————— ❖ —————

# The Real Adventure Begins

It is my deepest hope that this 21-day adventure will be just the beginning of your miraculous journey with the angels. Whatever you experienced during your time with them, big or small, know that the work you have accomplished here is absolutely priceless.

If you mostly had subtle experiences, I want to acknowledge that sometimes it is the minor shifts that are the most miraculous. A new sense of inner peace, a deepened relationship with Spirit, and even a newly cultivated daily spiritual practice are all monumental wins for your heart, mind, and soul.

A question that always comes up from participants at the end of these angel rituals is: "Now what do I do?" They essentially want to know how to keep going with the angels.

I love when people ask me this question, because these 21 days were actually not intended to be the end. They were meant to open the door for you to develop an ongoing, deep, and very real relationship with your angels.

No matter what happened for you over the past 21 days, if you want to keep rocking your angel magic, this last section will give you simple yet powerful steps that you can take to continue to intensify your relationship with these miraculous allies.

Remember now that the door is open. It will be up to you to take the lead and keep this angel adventure going. Here's how to keep the angel juju coming at you.

### Step 1: Sit with the Angels Daily

If you want to keep your angel magic flowing, then there is one thing that you should do no matter what. You should continue to sit with your angels daily.

Just like with any relationship, if you don't put in the energy, love, and attention that your connection with the angels deserves, the relationship will wither and become frail, and may eventually die.

I want you to continue to receive the benefits of love and healing from all the hard work you have put in, and in order for you to continue to reap those rewards, you will need to do your part.

You don't have to do a formal invocation or meditation every time, but creating a sacred time and space for you to commune with your angels each day will continue to strengthen your bond with them and will keep opening up your life to all kinds of flow and goodness.

If you don't want to think too hard about creating your own invocations, here are some easy steps for you to practice daily:

1. Secure a quiet space.
2. Call in the Creator and the angels.
3. Share with them your worries and concerns.
4. Tell the angels your desires and make your requests.
5. Listen for any intuitive guidance that they have for you that day.
6. Thank them and give them gratitude for all the awesomeness that is in your life already.

This format takes no more than 10 to 15 minutes a day and will support your life in beautiful ways.

### Step 2: Take Sacred Action Daily

Many folks have the wrong idea about angels. People often think that all they have to do is pray to the angels, and the angels will magically come and rescue them. That's not exactly how it works.

Yes, the angels are capable of working absolute miracles in your life just through prayer; however, it doesn't always work that way. Often there is a piece of the puzzle that has to be done on your end in order for this miracle to be fulfilled.

As you continue your journey, the angels will give you inspired ideas to help you solve all your biggest life problems, but they can't do the legwork for you.

It's absolutely up to you to take the steps that you are being guided to take if you want to massively improve the quality of your life, health, or wealth.

After all, you can't win the lottery if you sit on the couch all day watching TV and never go to the store to buy the lotto ticket. The same exact principle works for your dream life and the angels. If you want a new job but are mostly just praying about it or, even worse, sitting around and complaining about it, then it simply won't happen.

For every wish, dream, and desire that you have, there will always be actions steps that you are being guided to take. If you don't take those steps, your angel magic and your life will slow down and eventually stagnate.

With this concept in mind, I now want to ask you a couple of questions that might help you discern which actions to take.

- Over the past 21 days, what actions do you feel like you are being guided to take toward creating a better life for yourself?
- What repetitive thoughts, ideas, or inspirations have you had that might require you to take action?

Sometimes the guidance can be subtle, so it's up to you to slow down, reflect, and intercept the awesome solutions that are getting floated your way by your heavenly allies.

Your answers to the above questions, whatever they are, could be pure gold, but they can only be turned into gold if you take the steps necessary. Don't let your doubts fool you. Sometimes it takes an excessive amount of courage to listen to these beautiful whispers and actually do something about them. So let yourself be bold, and begin taking wild, big, beautiful actions toward realizing the life of your dreams. Your angels will be with you every step of the way.

### Step 3: Find a Like-Minded Community and Say No to Energy Vampires

In a world full of negativity, it is important to take a serious inventory of the folks in your life, and make sure that you have at least a few people in your circle who will support you on your journey toward living in more love, spirituality, healing, joy, happiness, and sheer awesomeness.

So many people that I've talked to from all around the world feel alone among their families or communities, and are often afraid of being judged for their blossoming spiritual beliefs. In order to address this, I want you to listen very closely to what I'm about to tell you. Here it is: *not everyone deserves access to your life.* I'll say it in a different way: *you are not obligated to keep people in your life who suck.* Be mindful of whom you let into your inner circle, because if they have a lot of bad juju, it will be difficult for you to keep up the positive energy and momentum that you have built over this time with the angels.

A large portion of your success in expanding your angel magic depends on your ability to set strong and consistent boundaries in your relationships. It's hard to live a miraculous life when you have a bunch of negative folks in it dragging you down, so do what you can to surround yourself with high-vibe, like-minded souls who understand you and will support your spiritual and life expansion.

If you have a hard time finding amazing people locally, there are plenty of amazing spiritual communities online. Feel free to check out my own angel-inspired online communities. You can find out more about them on my website at CorinGrillo.com.

We all need support in our lives, so please do ask your angels to help you find the right people who can support you, your dreams, and your blossoming connection with the angels and the divine.

## Step 4: Take Classes

If you loved this mystical approach to working with angels, then you will definitely love taking classes or workshops designed to help you open up your intuition and strengthen your relationship with the angels and the divine even further.

From teaching these kinds of classes over the years, I have seen incredible transformation happen for those people who continue to learn about their own spiritual gifts and the angels.

If you feel the call, I highly recommend you find classes that make your spiritual heart sing, so that you keep expanding in wisdom, knowledge, and experience with the angels.

## Step 5: Feel Gratitude, Gratitude, and More Gratitude

Last but definitely not least, the angels would like me to mention, yet again, the power of gratitude.

People are often ultra-clear on what's *not* working for them in their lives but rarely focus on what *is* working for them. We humans are masters at focusing on the lack in our lives. However, one of the biggest keys to success is simply realizing that you are already successful.

This is a big mindset shift for most of us, but when you train your mind to focus on what is going right in your life, you also naturally begin to align yourself with the energetic field of the miraculous. And guess who lives in the field of the miraculous? That's right, the angels.

Take this to heart, and work to attune your mind to the beauty and blessings in your life already. Think of your mind as if it were a radio dial, where you can instantly tune in to any station you like. If you continually tune your awareness to the "Gratitude" channel, versus the "Life Sucks" channel, the goodness in your life will expand, and so will your connection with the angels.

Make sure to give gratitude daily for your life as it is, and don't be afraid to share your gratitude with the people in your life whom you love the most.

## Before We Depart

I hope that these five steps will continue to support your personal discovery with the angels. So many miracle stories have been reported to me over the years from doing this work, and it is my true hope that your story will soon be one of them.

As we conclude our journey together, I want you to know that I am grateful that the angels have placed this book into your hands. Please keep doing your work with the angels, and may the angels continue to surround you with love, healing, hope, inspiration, support, abundance, and mega doses of miracles.

Always remember that there are no coincidences, that you are not alone, and that miracles are, in fact, real. The angels saved my life, and they can save yours too. *Let them.*

On angels' wings we fly together, never alone again.

Angel juju coming at you,
Corin

# Acknowledgments

This book came together thanks to a series of extraordinary events and the presence of even more extraordinary people.

I want to thank Jack Grillo for believing in me through the years, even when I didn't, and for being my anchor and my ground. Thank you also for helping me get this book ready for my publisher. You have been such a gift to me.

Thank you, Luci and Luna, for being such amazing children and for gracefully allowing me the time and space to wrangle this book together. You both make everything in my life so much sillier and so much better. You are my muses and my guiding lights.

Corey Eaton, thank you for all the love, support, and amazing adventures that you have brought to me during this writing journey. Your epic contribution to my life has been an absolute godsend.

To Lara Brightside and Kevin Heidt from Living Brightside Enterprises: Thank you for the marketing genius and the business support over the years and, most of all, for our friendship. Lara, a special thanks to you for introducing me to New World Library in the wild and synchronistic way in which that happened. I'm forever grateful.

To the team at New World Library: I'm in awe of the heart that each of you puts into your publishing work. Your enthusiasm about this book has meant the world to me. A special thanks to Marc Allen for the amazing cappuccino and for recommending that I submit this book. To Kim Corbin, my publicist at NWL, for your openness, support, and unicorn power in getting this book out there. And to Kristen Cashman for your badass editor's eagle eye and for your patience! Thank you to the rest of the team for helping this book become a reality. You are all such incredible humans, and I'm grateful the angels brought us together.

Thank you, Gwen Czura and Cari Bream, for the preliminary editing and research that you did to help me with the first submission of this book. You are both rockstars.

To the Red Fox Tribe and the Power Path, for your strength, support, and wisdom.

To Dad, Corrinne, and Noni: Thank you for the incredible influence that you've had in my life. I wouldn't be the human I am today without you.

To Mom: Been 30 years since you left your body, but I know you are still one of my biggest supporters. Thank you for being my angel.

To my students and clients around the world: Your

love and support take my breath away. Each of you is my own personal miracle.

Last but not least, thank you to the angels, the archangels, and my other invisible allies. The miracles you bring to my life continue to amaze me. Thank you for the guidance and courage you have given me over the years. And thank you for the magical pathways you have opened up to get this book into the hands of the people who need it most. You rule.

# About the Author

Corin Grillo, MA, LMFT, is a licensed psychotherapist, speaker, healer, teacher, and workshop leader. A miracle saved her life, cured her of lifelong depression, and awakened her spiritual gifts. Since that day, Corin has been committed to teaching others about the profound magic that lives inside them and how to set it free with the help of the angels.

Corin is also the founder of the Angel Alchemy Academy. She teaches by offering others down-to-earth spiritual wisdom, ritual, and powerful energy medicine that awaken the heart, mind, and soul and often facilitate direct mystical experiences.

You can learn more about Corin's work and join her angel community at CorinGrillo.com.